U0964178

新国标应用型本科商务英语系列教材

总主编　王立非

商务礼仪实训
（双语）（第二版）
Practical Business Etiquette
(Second Edition)

主　编　刘艳萍　石丽云　郑晶晶
副主编　唐　妮　齐真珍　周　泽　李　静
编　者　骆蔓莉　梁　婧　杨逢春　吴志平

对外经济贸易大学出版社
中国·北京

图书在版编目（CIP）数据

商务礼仪实训：双语 / 刘艳萍，石丽云，郑晶晶主编. -- 2 版. -- 北京 : 对外经济贸易大学出版社, 2024. 7. -- （新国标应用型本科商务英语系列教材 / 王立非总主编）. -- ISBN 978-7-5663-2627-0

Ⅰ. F718

中国国家版本馆 CIP 数据核字第 20244UX521 号

商务礼仪实训（双语）（第二版）

Practical Business Etiquette (Second Edition)

刘艳萍　石丽云　郑晶晶　主编

责任编辑：钟　平

出版发行：对外经济贸易大学出版社
社　　址：北京市朝阳区惠新东街 10 号
网　　址：www.uibep.com
资源网址：www.uibepresources.com
邮政编码：100029
邮购电话：010－64492338
发行部电话：010－64492342
E-mail：uibep@126.com

成品尺寸：185mm×260mm
印　　张：12.5
字　　数：289 千字
ISBN 978-7-5663-2627-0
印　　刷：北京时代华都印刷有限公司
版　　次：2024 年 7 月北京第 2 版
印　　次：2024 年 7 月第 1 次印刷
定　　价：49.00 元

新国标应用型本科商务英语系列教材

编　委　会

出版说明

党的二十大报告指出，中国积极参与全球治理体系改革和建设，践行共商共建共享的全球治理观，推动全球治理朝着更加公正合理的方向发展。中国呼吁世界各国弘扬全人类共同价值，促进各国人民相知相亲，尊重世界文明多样性，以文明交流超越文明隔阂、文明互鉴超越文明冲突、文明共存超越文明优越，共同应对各种全球性挑战。

习近平总书记强调，要大力培养掌握党和国家方针政策、具有全球视野、通晓国际规则、熟练运用外语、精通中外谈判和沟通的国际化人才。

教材是实现人才培养的基本工具和载体。“新国标应用型本科商务英语系列教材”是应对全球挑战、有效进行国际商务沟通、顺应国家现代教育改革的必然要求。2014 年 6 月 22 日国务院发布《关于加快发展现代职业教育的决定》（以下简称《决定》），全面部署加快发展现代职业教育。《决定》指出要“采取试点推动、示范引领等方式，引导一批普通本科高等学校向应用技术类型高等学校转型，重点举办本科职业教育”。

截至 2022 年 8 月，全国有 429 所高等院校开设了商务英语本科专业，其中多数院校属于应用型本科院校。本系列教材结合商务英语语言和教学的特点，融合多年商务英语教学实践，由长期从事商务英语教学一线的专家倾力打造，适用于全国应用型本科商务英语专业和财经类本科专业学生。

本套教材具有以下特色：

一、吸收二语习得和现代教育的最新理论，体现《商务英语专业本科教学质量国家标准》的最新要求。教材编写上注重提高学生的语言技能、让学生掌握相关的商务知识与实践技能，培养学生的跨文化交际能力、思辨与创新能力，以及自主学习能力。

二、秉承应用型本科教育“优化理论，突出实践”的理念。应用型本科教育注重技术但不能完全抛弃学术，其人才培养是学术性与职业性的有机统一，其基本特征是“本科底蕴+突出应用+专业特长”。体现在教材上，它强调“优化理论，突出实践”，优化理论基础，注重理论与专业技术的相关性，以培养目标与从业要求为依据对基础理论进行优化整合，介绍与专业相关的必要理论，重点强化行业知识的讲解；突出实践方面，强调教材的编排设计从教学目标到内容的组织，练习题的设计都环环相扣、注重培养学生的职业适应能力，突出实践教学的内涵。

三、贯彻“任务引领、项目导向”的指导思想。本套教材以“任务驱动”为理念，强化了教材的任务驱动效应，突出作业流程的可操作性；以真实企业业务经营为主线贯穿始终，从而保持教材内容前后的一致性和连续性；通过具体任务的设计和实施，使学生能够掌握业务技能。

对外经济贸易大学出版社

2024 年 1 月

鸣　谢

本教材中的所有插图和视频是在广西财经学院商务外国语学院和国际教育学院的老师和同学以及社会热心人士的支持和协助下完成的。特对所有参与本书内容拍摄和制作的人员表示衷心的感谢。

（按姓氏拼音顺序排列）

1. 形象：

蔡金芮、陈爱文、陈伯儒、陈聪、党唯铭、邓东金、邓林君、范杰洪、何菲菲、黄吴彩虹、黄伊、黄依莹、胡晨曦、胡强、酒昭睿、黎若诗、李翠梅、李荷、李静、李资鉴、梁冰冰、梁春雯、林依粤、廖蒋菲、廖展威、刘敏、龙丽琴、罗金铭、莫海涛、莫嘉琪、莫心妍、农细娜、欧小燕、潘伟鹏、彭轲、覃琪琪、苏健、苏宇、齐真珍、韦玲玲、韦宁、吴子娴、杨焯杰、余文东、张昊琪、郑晶晶、郑晓丹、周唐贤苑、朱文海、Mr. Sterling、Ms. Turner

2. 拍摄：

陈英、刘明、吴志平、吴祚超、张昊琪、赵骏溪、周泽

3. 绘画：

洪杰、罗嘉楹、石丽云、石敏、谭淳宇、许一帆、周炜程

4. 图片：

梁小燕、莫芬、刘艳萍、石丽云、石翔云、郑晶晶

5. 视频：

班佳晨、陈筱琪、邓林君、邓宗怡、胡慧初、花蕾、黄秋红、蒋勇玉、李资鉴、梁帆、梁爽林子、梁晓艳、刘艳、刘洋、陆斌、罗义婷、莫佳美、莫丽颖、莫小萍、潘少华、庞丽、庞绪方、彭轲、覃梦圆、苏元善、谭凯芳、唐紫依、韦建平、谢理朝、杨芊芊、殷诗梦、玉雪、张育华、朱世杰

6. 微课：

李劼全、石丽云、郑晶晶

Preface 前　言

在"一带一路"倡议的提出和中国企业"走出去"的背景下，中国企业与世界各国的经济往来和商务活动日趋频繁和密切。国际商务活动对具有专业素质和跨文化意识的商务人才的需求在不断增加。商务礼仪是体现商务专业素质和跨文化交流能力的一个重要方面。无论是对准备从事商务工作的在校学生，还是职场中的商务人士来说，学会与人相处的技巧、拥有得体的仪态，掌握日常接待、商务会见、商务宴请等涉外活动的礼仪要求，对个人事业成功起着至关重要的作用，也是个人素质以及本国文化的重要体现。《商务礼仪实训（双语）》这本教材正是针对以上背景与需求而编写的。

本教材以习近平新时代中国特色社会主义思想为指导，以教育部制订的《高等学校外国语言文学类教学质量国家标准》和《普通高等学校本科外国语言文学类专业教学指南》为指导，落实立德树人根本任务，寓价值塑造于知识传授和能力培养之中，帮助学生树立正确的世界观、价值观和人生观。教材旨在通过丰富的商务文化礼仪技能培训，提高学习者商务沟通能力，提升个人职业形象，从而培养具有家国情怀，具备国际化视野，通晓国际规则，熟练使用外语进行商务沟通、协作和谈判的高素质国际化复合型人才，最终做好国际传播和国际商务合作，更好地服务于国家和区域社会发展。

本教材帮助学习者掌握与国际商务礼仪相关的基本知识、规则和技巧；通晓商务活动各个环节中的礼仪和规范；了解中外文化差异。通过商务礼仪技能训练，帮助学习者遵循商务交往的惯例与客户沟通；运用礼仪知识处理问题、应对特殊情境；具有思辨创新的能力；举止得体，展现出良好的职业道德和职业素养。教材同时有机融入社会主义核心价值观和集体主义精神；关注个人鉴赏力和审美素质，关注生态文明；强调礼仪意识、敬业精神及社会责任感。

本教材由四大模块构成，模块一为礼仪概述，模块二为仪容仪表，模块三为通用商务交往礼仪，模块四为商务场合特定礼仪，包括着装礼仪、见面礼仪、介绍礼仪、交谈话题、餐桌礼仪、乘车礼仪、行进礼仪、赠礼礼仪、面试礼仪、商务谈判、商务宴请、会务礼仪等方面。每个章节包含教学目标、礼仪知识、案例分析、课后练习等内容。较全面地涵盖了职场中商务人士所必须掌握和了解的形象要求和各种行为规范。

本教材第一版于2019年出版，在使用的四年过程中，各位教师和学生对此教材提出了宝贵的意见和建议。2023年，教材增加了7位编者，对第一版内容进行了修订，增加了礼仪概述模块，补充了中国传统服饰、赠礼礼仪、行进礼仪、乘车礼仪等内容，丰富了课后阅读材料和课后练习。同时，教材积极与时俱进，在各章节中补充并突出社会主义核心价值观的培养，强调涉外商务工作者诚信、公正、友善等职业素养，弘扬仁、义、礼、智、信的中国优秀传统文化。如在中国传统服饰部分突出了文化自信，仪态礼仪和着装礼仪部分强调展现个人审美、塑造良好的个人形象；会面礼仪、握手礼仪和电话礼仪部分侧重学生个人职业素养的培养；谈判礼仪和乘车礼仪部分强调爱国、诚实、守信等社会主义核心价值观；求职面试礼仪着重突出对理想信念的追求；用餐礼仪和赠礼礼仪融入生态文明和社会责任感教育，强调环保意识和职业道德。

本教材以英文为主，辅以部分中文解释和辅助说明，设置了形式多样的课前导入练习，强调实际操作的课后巩固练习，并配以丰富的图片，提供微课、二维码扫码观看视频或网站链接等生动直观的材料以激发学生的学习兴趣，有利于学生的课后复习，同时也能培养学生的自学能力。为了便于学习，有些练习配有参考答案；有些练习属于开放式的问题，则没有提供参考答案，需要学习者自行思考回答。本教材适合英语专业、商务英语专业、国际贸易、国际商务、翻译等涉外专业大学生使用，也可以供政府、企业相关部门的商务培训所用。

本教材集中了长期从事该课程教学的一线教师的宝贵经验，在广西财经学院商务英语专业、英语专业和法语专业连续四年的使用中不断获得反馈和完善中修订而成。教材由外教 Nickolas Miew Sing Su 审稿校订，在此一并致谢。由于编者水平有限，教材难免还存在许多问题，诚望教师朋友们不吝赐教，提出宝贵意见。

Contents 目 录

Module One Etiquette Overview 礼仪概述

Module Two Attire and Grooming 仪容仪表

Module Three Etiquette in Business Contact 交往礼仪

Module One
Etiquette Overview
礼仪概述

Etiquette Overview

礼仪概述

学习任务

1. 何为“礼”？
2. 为何要学“礼”？

Etiquette is a kind of moral code and social consciousness. It is a specific form and basic skill to show respect to others. Business etiquette is the code of conduct that people use in business activities to maintain their corporate or personal images and show respect and friendliness to their associates.

礼者，敬人也，仪者，形式也。商务礼仪是人们在商务活动中，用以维护企业或个人形象，对交往对象表示尊重、友好的行为规范。

Warm-up:

1. Q&A:

Lewis Hamilton (刘易斯·汉密尔顿，F1 赛车手) was banned from Wimbledon’s Centre Court’s Royal Box in 2015 when he was invited to watch Novak Djokovic (诺瓦克·德约科维奇，网球运动员) take on the mighty Roger Federer (罗杰·费德勒，网球运动员). Discuss with your classmates to figure out the most possible reason for which he was banned from the Royal Box?

A. He was talking loudly in the Royal Box.

B. He turned up late to watch the match.

C. He wasn’t wearing a jacket or tie.

D. He wore a distracting hat in the Royal Box.

Background information:

Wimbledon

Wimbledon, officially known as The Championships, is the most prestigious among the four Grand Slam tennis tournaments. It has been held at the All England Club in Wimbledon, London, since 1877. The tournament is renowned for its unique traditions, such as players wearing all-white attire.

The Royal Box

The Royal Box is a special seating section at Center Court of Wimbledon. It is reserved primarily for members of the Royal Family, other dignitaries, and VIP guests. Access to the Royal Box is by invitation only, and those fortunate enough to be seated there are expected to adhere to some strict etiquette rules.

2. Discuss the following question with your partner.

China is an etiquette nation, and ancient Chinese culture is the culture of "*Li* (礼)". How should people combine Chinese etiquette with the times to carry forward Chinese excellent traditional culture, and strengthen cultural self-confidence?

Keywords: New media; Family; Schools; Society

I. What Is Etiquette? 何为礼

Contents:

1. Definition
2. Origin
3. Connotation

Etiquette is a code of behaviors and manners that are considered polite, respectful or socially acceptable in a particular culture, society or group. Etiquette can vary greatly among cultures and regions. It's important to be aware of local customs and norms when interacting with people from different backgrounds.

Business etiquette is the application and embodiment of general etiquette in business activities. Learning business etiquette has become an important means for enterprises to improve reputation and enhance competitiveness.

不学礼，无以立。

1. Definition

Cambridge Dictionary defines etiquette as "the set of rules and customs that control accepted behavior in particular social group or social situation".

In English, etiquette means the practices and forms prescribed by social convention or by authority.

礼仪是礼节、仪式的统称。指在人际交往中，自始至终以一定的、约定俗成的程序、方式来表现的律己、敬人的完整行为。（金正昆，2013）

2. Origin

2.1 The origin of Chinese etiquette

Chinese etiquette originated in the middle and late primitive society. Ancient Chinese worship and their sacrifice to the heaven were considered to be one of the origins of Chinese etiquette, as well as the social customs. Etiquette is not created by any person, but is formed in the social interaction among people, and it is uniformly observed and used by everyone.

中华礼仪起源于祭祀和风俗习惯。

2.2 The origin of Western etiquette

In the West, the term "etiquette" originated from the French word "Etiquette", meaning "a pass to the court".

In order to ensure the order of activities in the court, ancient France issued a pass printed with court discipline to everyone entering the court as the rule and code of conduct. Later, the word "Etiquette" came into English and evolved into the meaning of "etiquette" (礼仪) which became the rules and guidelines that people should follow in their communication. International etiquette originates from Western etiquette. The history of Western civilization also fully reflects the history of human's pursuit of etiquette.

3. Connotation of Etiquette

Etiquette is recognized as the code of conduct for coordinating interpersonal relations, which is embodied in politeness, courtesy and ceremony.

3.1 Politeness

Politeness generally refers to the words and deeds that people show friendliness, humility and respect to each other in social communication. Politeness focuses on the expression of people's quality and accomplishment, and its external expression includes two aspects, namely polite language and polite behavior. Polite language is honorifics, a verbal language in a way of being kind and appropriate in social settings. Polite behavior refers to non-verbal language, including one's appearance and posture, etc.

Politeness reflects the moral fashion of the times and people's cultural level and degree of civilization. Politeness in mutual communication not only reflects the relationship of mutual respect and friendly cooperation between people, but also helps to regulate the mutual relationship among people and avoiding some unnecessary personal contradictions and conflicts.

礼貌一般是指人们在社会交往中所表现出的友好、谦让、尊重对方的言行举止，包括礼貌语言和礼貌行为。

3.2 Courtesy

Courtesy is the customary form of polite behavior that people use to show respect and friendliness in the process of communication, such as shaking hands, bowing, greeting, hugging and so on. It is the concrete embodiment of politeness in the aspects of appearance, manners, language and behavior. Courtesy develops differently in each country or nation, and changes with the progress of the times. Therefore, it is necessary to learn about courtesy of various countries and nations in order to show respect to their customs in the process of mutual communication.

礼节是人们在交往过程中和交往场合中表现出尊重和友善的礼貌行为的习惯形式。

3.3 Ceremony

Ceremony is a formal order form of etiquette to show respect or solemnization. It is held on a certain occasion with special etiquette procedures of standardized activities. Due to different purposes, the ceremonies are also diverse, including signing ceremony, opening ceremony, closing ceremony, award ceremony and so on. As a form of expressing politeness and courtesy, ceremony plays an important role in etiquette.

仪式是一种更为正式的礼节秩序形式。它是在特定的场合举行的，具有特殊礼仪程序的规范化活动。

II. Significance and Characteristics of Etiquette 礼的意义和特征

Nowadays, it is an era highlighting etiquette. Etiquette plays a vital role, reflecting a person's basic quality, social interaction as well as interpersonal relations.

美国现代成功学大师拿破仑·希尔说："世界上最廉价，而且能得到最大收益的一项物质，就是礼节。"

1. Significance

Etiquette is of great significance. Etiquette is good for individual development in many ways, such as awakening human dignity, promoting people's self-discipline and shaping their personality. Besides, being in line with the idea of "politeness makes peace", etiquette plays an important role in handling various complex interpersonal relationships promoting social development in a harmonious and stable way.

Business etiquette will make you:

Polite	Elegant
Professional	Popular

2. Characteristics of Etiquette

In the same historical period, different countries and nations have different etiquette norms. Although there are differences in the content of etiquette, its basic characteristics are consistent, mainly in the following five aspects.

2.1 Standardization

The standardization of etiquette refers to the certain standards and norms of etiquette in interpersonal communication. The formation of etiquette norms is a behavior pattern formed by people in interpersonal communication practice and fixed by certain customs and traditional ways, which reflects the requirements of contemporary society and is generally followed by people's code of conduct.

2.2 Inheritance

Etiquette norms solidify the conventional procedures in people's communication activities, which are inherited as time goes on and form the characteristics of inheritance. People should adopt the attitude of taking the essence, discarding the dregs and make use of the past for the present.

2.3 Difference

Etiquette norms will vary depending on time, space or object. The application of etiquette depends on the time, place, occasion, object and so on. Different requirements and restrictions may be applied due to various circumstances.

俗话说："到什么山唱什么歌。"

2.4 Epochal character

In essence, etiquette is a product of social and historical development, with distinct characteristics of the times. On the one hand, it is formed and developed in the practice of human long-term communicative activities. It can never be completely divorced from a specific historical context. On the other hand, with the development of society and the progress of history, the emergence of new problems of social activities requires etiquette to change with the times to adapt to the new requirements.

Exercise 章节练习

Discussion 1:

Try to use the basic knowledge of etiquette to talk about your feelings about Chinese historical story of "负荆请罪" (voluntarily offer to be punished with the rod).

Discussion 2:

How to understand "礼，时为大"？What does this sentence have to do with promoting economic development of China?

TIPS: Seize the opportunity.
Pay attention to the construction of corporate culture.

Module Two
Attire and Grooming
仪容仪表

Chapter One

Dress Etiquette 着装礼仪

学习任务

1. 了解职场着装的 TPO（Time，Place，Occasion）原则。
2. 了解职场着装的特点和要求。
3. 如何根据不同场合选择不同的着装。

Dress: A Kind of Social Symbol

I. Women’s Dress 女士着装

Contents:

1. TPO Principle
2. Four rules for women professionals
3. Dress code
4. Extra suggestions
5. Traditional attire

Warm-up:

What is the girl’s plan for today?

Apparel makes the man.

—Quote

1. TPO Principle

TPO is the abbreviation word of **Time, Place, Occasion,** which means that people's dressing should be appropriate with this rule.

时间　　场所　　地点

1.1 Time

一年有四季，人们常常根据季节、气候的变化选择不同的服装。一天有 24 小时，在不同的时间节点，不同的事件场景下，人们也会做着不同的事情，着装也会有所改变。所以，服饰的选择无法完全取决于个人喜好，所谓的“我喜欢”也不能成为选择的标准。

Warm and high-quality woolen skirt would be nice in winter; clothes in summer should be light but made of non-transparent quality.

1.2 Place

不论是室外还是室内，五星级酒店还是菜市场，职场还是家里，你的服装要符合地点的变化。

Dressing should change according to places. When you entertain visitors at home, comfortable and tidy casual wear is appropriate. If the visit occurs in the company, suits make you look more professional. When you travel around, local traditions and customs should be taken into consideration.

1.3 Occasion

对于不同的场合，如拜访顾客和听音乐会，出席晚宴和到朋友家吃饭，没有人会穿一样的衣服，因为实在太怪异了。

Serious and official dressing is required when you meet clients and attend meetings. When attending official banquet, woman usually chooses Chinese traditional cheongsam (Qipao) and long evening gowns. What would it be like if everyone dresses lightly, but you wear an evening dress?

There is a general summary for women's dressing code: suits, skirt/business dress, and uniforms are appropriate on business occasion. While in a social occasion, evening dress or fashionable dress that emphasizes personal style is the good choice. For casual occasion, you can wear any clothes that make you feel comfortable. Such clothes as sportswear, jeans and casual wear will be nice. However, can women's dress be summarized by some simple words?

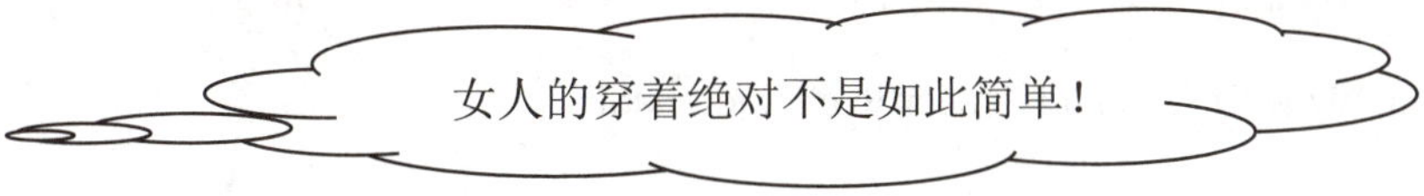

An investigation by www.zhaopin.com shows that there are standards for women's dressing.

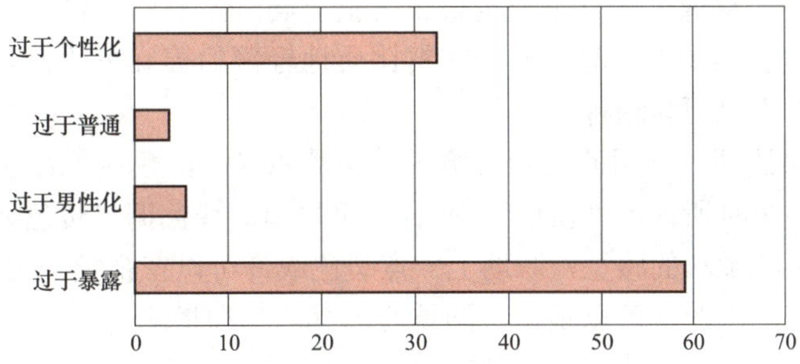

你觉得最不合适的职场女装是什么样的？

A story:

At the beginning of this year, I asked the students to put on the clothes that they thought appropriate for the interview in a volunteer training session. But the students' dressing knocked me down. More than 80% students had no idea what the appropriate clothes are. Some of them were in jeans and sneakers; others were in pink Barbie-like skirt or mini-skirt. I told them "It is beautiful, but inappropriate for the interview." Then students asked "what are the appropriate clothes?" Indeed, that was an important question. Appropriate clothing is a matter of personal preference.

服饰告诉了人们你内心的想法，同时决定了人们对你的第一印象。

Dressing is a big deal of image presentation. Western fashion designers believe that "clothes can't make a person perfect, but 80% of the first impression comes from dressing." For the graduates who are going to get their first jobs, the point should be the workwear. To present a professional, confident, authorized image in business, graduates should start from dressing.

2. Four Rules for Women Professionals

In such important occasions as a critical meeting, a ceremony, or an official banquet, women should dress appropriately, and pay attention to the following rules:

2.1 Avoiding clothes that are:

too bright
too clutter
too revealing
too short
too transparent
too tight
too fashionable with extremely specific characteristics

款式、材质、颜色、风格都会帮你与人进行交流，让别人了解你的内心。选择服饰并不能仅凭价格，昂贵或者便宜不一定代表质量。同时，衣服的材质不同给人带来的感觉也不同，比如，材料硬挺不易褶皱的衣料比质地轻薄的棉麻更适合职场，有时无须熨烫平整就可穿着，而且更显精神。

色彩是一个魔法师，不同的色彩会给人不同的感受，深色调或冷色调会让人产生视觉上的收缩感，即平时所说的“显瘦”，而且庄重严肃；浅色调或暖色调的服装会有扩张感，却给人带来温暖柔和的感觉，职场上一点暖色或许可以在视觉上削弱“攻击性”，有时甚至可事半功倍。因此，可以根据不同需要进行选择和搭配。

In addition to clothing, shoes, stockings and groves also deserve special attention. For example, a pair of transparent stockings that align with your clothes will be a good choice, while a pair of stockings with patterns can not ascend the place of refinement. In an official and grave occasion, it is inappropriate to wear sandals or boots, but a pair of black leather shoes is most widely chosen and matches any clothes. A pair of kitten heels without open toes is considered as a safe choice for business occasions. Is there anything should be paid special attention to?

2.2 Suit dress—The most suitable clothes for women professionals

Generally, requirements are as follows:

2.2.1 Suit

Good texture: smooth, clean, soft, stiff, well-pressed, wrinkle-free, no pilling, lint-free

Less color: cool tone, less than two colors, presenting an elegant, decent, solemn (i.e. black, navy, taupe, gray, burgundy wine)

No fancy patterns: no patterns or with grid, spot, stripes

Less decoration

Proper size: Tops should not be too long and skirts should not be too short.

Suitable styles: "H""X""A""Y"

Fashionable style: Collars, buttons, flies, groves, sleeves and skirts should be trendy.

搭配颜色较深、较为硬朗感的西服外套，衬衫面料要求轻薄而柔软，可选择真丝、麻纱、纯棉。色彩要求大方典雅，忌过于花里胡哨，可衬托女性柔和端庄。

2.2.2 Skirt

裙子：以包裙、窄裙为主，女性裙长宜在膝盖上下。年轻女性的裙子下摆可在膝盖以上 3 厘米～6 厘米，但不可太短；管理层或稍年长女性（30 岁以上）建议裙子应在膝盖以下 3 厘米左右。裙子太短不端庄，太长不够干净利落，会弱化职业感。

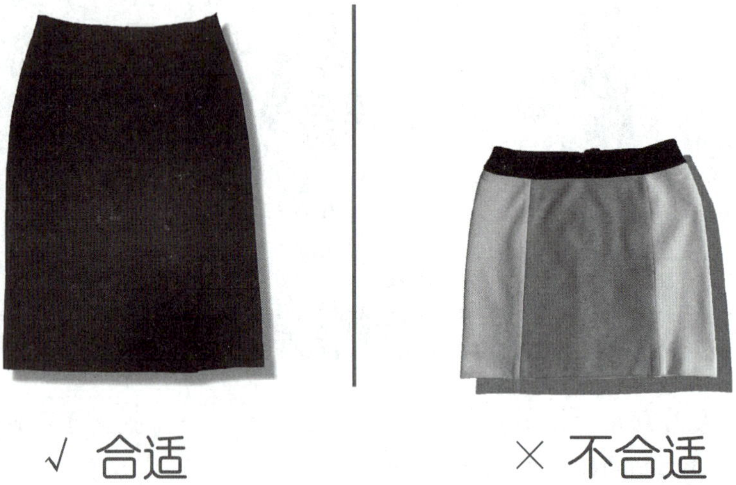

2.2.3 Shirt

衬衫：以单色为最佳之选。衬衫色彩与套裙的色彩协调，内深外浅或内浅外深，形成深浅对比。最好无图案。衬衫之内应当穿着内衣，但不可显露出来。

Attention:

1) Tuck the well-buttoned shirt into the skirt.

2) Don't take off your suit jacket in the formal occasions.

3) The shirt you wear in front of people should not be transparent or tight.

2.2.4 Shoes and socks

著名作家李碧华说过："看一个男人的品位，要看他的袜子。"那么，这句话似乎也可以理解为："看一个女人的品位，要看她的鞋子。"

鞋袜款式应以简单为主，颜色应与西装套裙相搭配。腿较粗的人适合穿深色的袜子，腿较细的人适合穿浅色的袜子。一般不要选择鲜艳、带有网格或有明显花纹的丝袜。

—Height of the heel on the shoes: about 3-5 cm.

—Suitable colors include neutral, black, beige, gray.

—The stockings and pantyhose are suitable.

Attention:

1) Skirts should come with stockings and pantyhose.
2) The suitable colors include skin and black.
3) Shoes should go well with stockings.
4) Shoes and stockings should be in perfect condition.
5) Don't wear ankle socks at will.
6) Don't take off shoes and stockings in public.
7) Stockings should not be revealed outside of the skirt or trousers.

3. Dress Code

Westerners are strict in dress code on different occasions. There are clear notifications for dress code in business banquet invitations, which helps people get prepared for the occasion. In this part, three rules for women will be introduced.

3.1 Business formal/power suit

Generally, formal dresses in business are suitable for some professional industries, such as finance, insurance, trade, education or service which are more conservative than others.

着装：整套的正规深色系西装，女士一般为西装筒裙，裙长盖膝，上身内搭衬衫（可为浅色）。

注意事项：衣服材质尽量避免含麻或全棉，容易起皱；女性可加入配饰增添亲和力。

3.2 Business semi-formal

Business semi-formals are appropriate for public relation, human resources and other general industry.

3.3 Business casual/smart casual

Generally, the staff in the positions where they don't meet clients may choose wearing such kind of dress. There are more styles, colors and texture for them to choose from.

着装要求：款式和颜色需正式又不失随和。某些公司的周五便装日即给员工穿着此类型服装。可出现三种颜色，建议使用渐进色。

3.4 Banquets

What should I wear for a banquet? The following part will answer this question. Generally, there are two ways of dressing in a social banquet as mentioned before.

3.4.1 Swallow tail/white tie

Time: 晚间六点以后

Place: 重大活动晚宴、正式晚宴、社交舞会等

Occasion: 极其正式隆重

Lady's dress: 长礼服（Evening Gown）

3.4.2 Tuxedo/black tie

Time: 晚六点后

Place: 重大庆典、正式宴会、节日派对以及商会、产品发布会等

Occasion: 正式场合

Lady's dress: 长短礼服裙皆可（long or short evening gown）

Attention:

If there is no dress code notified in the invitation, women professions can dress according to the requirements of business formal.

4. Extra Suggestions

Besides the requirements of dress for women professionals introduced in previous part, extra suggestions will be given as follows.

4.1 Bag

The importance of a bag to a woman is like a belt to a man, which greatly impresses people. Therefore, the texture of a bag is very important.

1）正式场合尽量不使用布包、铆钉包、双肩包，正式的皮质提包更好。

2）请根据场合的不同选择不同大小的皮包，休闲场合可选大型包（水桶包、斜挎包、大手提包），职场可选中型包（肩包、手提包），社交宴会可选小型包（手腕包、晚宴包、手拿包）。小型包精巧雅致，多选用毛皮（人造）、皮革、丝绒、金银丝混纺材料，用镶嵌、绣、编等工艺结合制作而成，华丽精巧是晚礼服用包的共同特点。

正装包

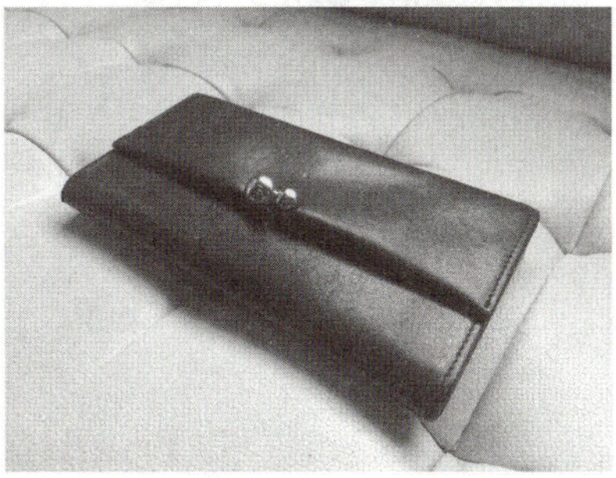

手包

4.2 Accessories

Make perfect accessories when preparing for social banquet, such as patterned silk scarf, chains, and glittering earrings. Simple earrings and necklace are suitable for workplace. You can choose some high-quality pearl, sapphire, emerald, or diamond accessories.

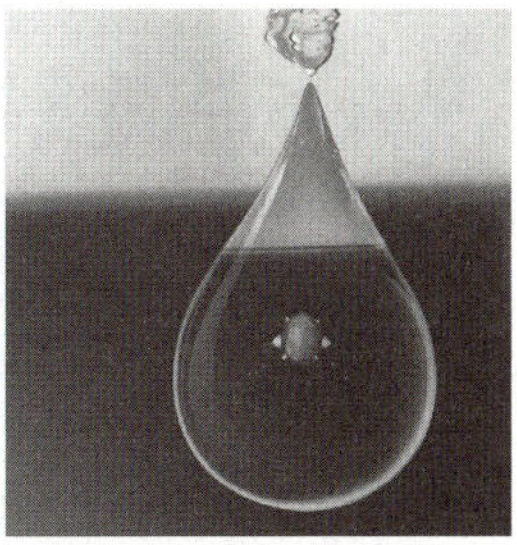

4.3 Scarf

Scarf should be solemn and dignified. The colors of scarf should present personal preference, the overall style and fashion trend. It is better to choose a scarf without any patterns or with elegant and solemn patterns.

4.4 Perfume

Ms. Coco Chanel once said that a woman who doesn't wear perfume has no future. In workplace, Eau de toilette with floral flavor is more favorable than perfume, which shows the softness of a woman. However, don't wear perfume on a plane, a hospital, a church or an interview.

5. Traditional Attire

5.1 Cheongsam (Qipao)

Cheongsam is a kind of typical ethnic costume that harmonizes and unifies both internally and externally. It is a representative of Chinese clothing culture, a traditional costume for Chinese women, and one of the most splendid phenomena and forms in China's long-standing clothing culture. It is known as the quintessence of Chinese culture and national costume for Chinese women.

旗袍被誉为“中国国粹”和“女性国服”，1984年被国务院指定为女性外交人员礼服。

旗袍是中国文化的一个浓缩符号，含蓄地表达着女性的美和魅力。传统的设计细节，张扬出更多女性特有的优雅魅力，彰显着中国服饰的雅韵之美。旗袍被作为一种具有民族代表意义的正式礼服出现在各种国际社交礼仪场合，被当作尊贵的会客礼仪服饰。

Over the past decade or so, cheongsam has made frequent appearances on the international fashion stage and has been seen as a formal dress with national significance in various international social etiquette occasions. There are a few things that people should pay attention to when wearing cheongsam.

Attention:

1) The fabric, color and style of the cheongsam should be coordinated with the occasion.
2) Button up all the buttons on cheongsam.
3) Cheongsam should be paired with pantyhose.
4) When wearing cheongsam, special attention should be paid to maintaining good posture.

出席节庆典礼，外事访问，隆重会议，婚礼宴会等正式场合，应选择面料高档、款式庄重的旗袍，发型、配饰、丝袜、皮包、高跟鞋等配件，都要与旗袍搭配。

5.2 The horse face skirt (Mamian skirt)

The horse face skirt (Mamian skirt) was one of the main skirt styles for women in ancient China. It was favored by people of several dynasties because of its unique functional and aesthetic style. The horse face skirt has experienced a series of style change since its origin in Song Dynasty, and the "skirt panel" takes strong root.

The horse face skirt is rich in colors and patterns, from dragons and phoenixes to curling auspicious cloud, all of which are the typical Chinese style. In some formal occasions, if dressed properly, the horse face skirt not only showcases the beauty of the East, but also demonstrates our confidence in traditional Chinese culture.

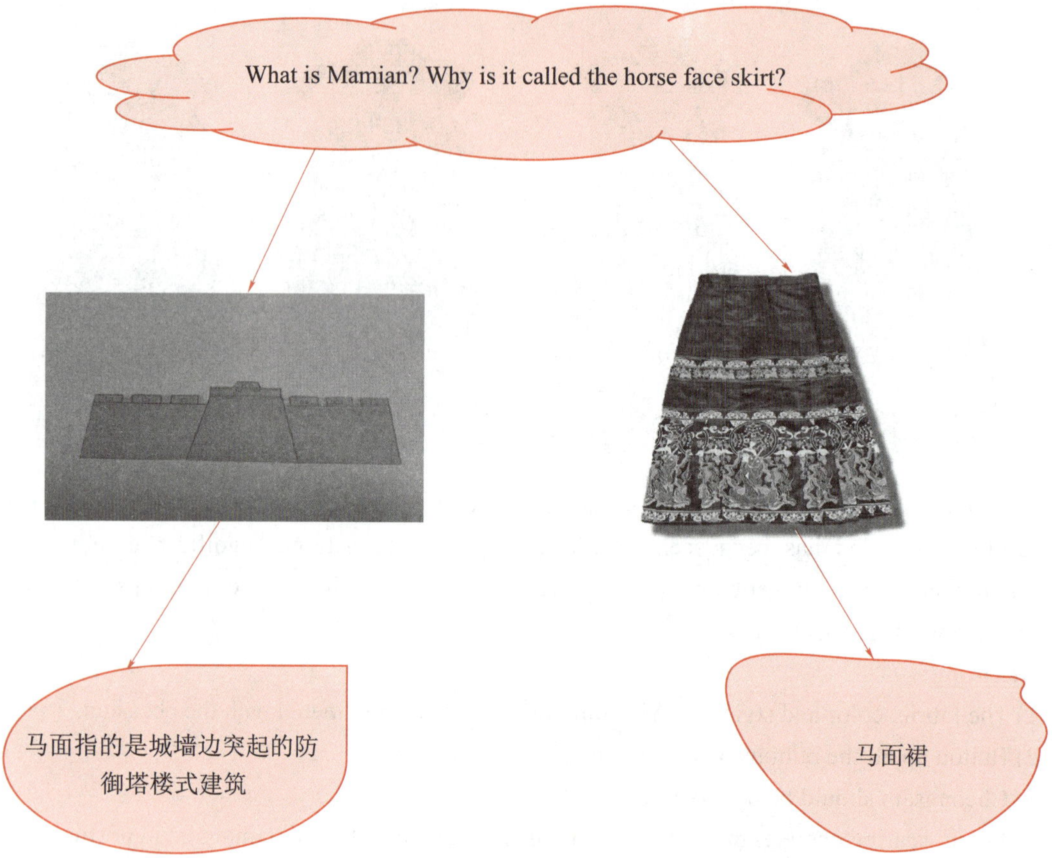

Wearing suggestions:

1) 裙长优选九分或者全长。
2) 款式优选纯色加印花叠加。
3) 选准尺码，腰围合身。

Ways of wearing the horse face skirt:

第一步：中间裙门对准身体正中间，左右裙门在后腰交叠；
第二步：将系带在后腰交叉，然后绕至身体正前方；
第三步：系带较长，可多缠绕一个圈，在左侧或者右侧打成蝴蝶结；
第四步：将蝴蝶结的耳朵藏在系带下面（根据个人习惯也可不藏蝴蝶结耳朵）。
（市面上的马面裙主要有无孔和打孔两种，穿法略有不同，不管是哪种款式都要注意保持裙门不歪，腰身平整。）

II. Men's Dress 男士着装

Contents:

1. Formal business attire
2. Informal business attire
3. Social dress
4. Traditional attire

Warm-up:

Q1: What are their plans for today?

Q2: What's their first impression on you? Please list three points you focus on most.

1. Formal Business Attire

1.1 Business suit

Business attire for man usually refers to suits. Suits are considered as the most popular and most frequently worn in workplace. Suits are various in textures, colors, styles, matching with shirt, neck tie or bow tie, constituting a well-grounded and dignified business suits.

男士商务着装通常应遵循“三色原则”：即身上的穿戴，包括公文包，不宜超过三种颜色。

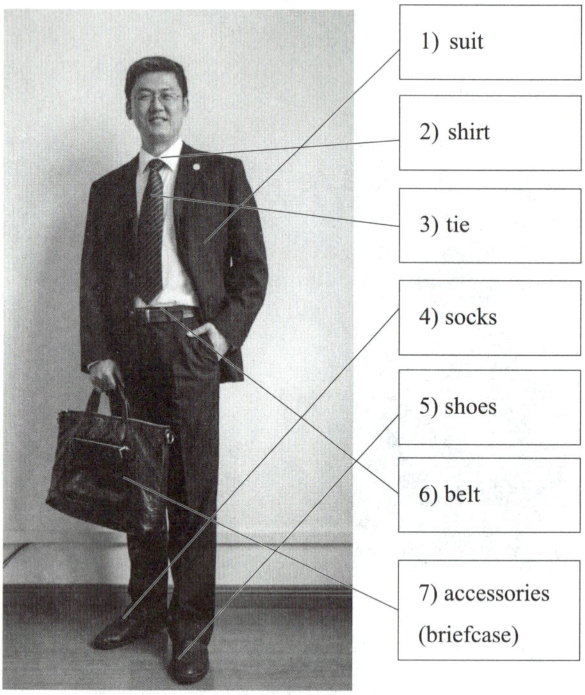

1.1.1 Suit

A high-quality, substantial, and delicately matched suit presents a man's elegance and efficiency. Meanwhile, it is a symbol of identity and taste. The following points should be taken into consideration when choosing a suit.

Textures: cotton, wool

Colors: cool colors (navy, gray, brown)

Styles: twinset/three-piece suit

single-breasted suit (with 1/2/3 breast buttons)/double-breasted suit

Attention:

1) 穿着前拆除袖口商标。

2) 除就座时解开西装上衣纽扣，其余时间应系好。

单排扣：“扣上不扣下”

（两粒扣款系上扣，三粒扣款系中扣或上、中扣）

双排扣：全部系好

3) 注意西裤的拉链要拉好。

4) 口袋里少装东西，物品应放入公文包中。

Three-piece suit with two buttons

Double-piece suit with one button

Double-piece suit with three buttons

Double-breasted suit

西装套装有不同分类方法：

● 两件套和三件套

两件套：上衣加西裤

三件套：上衣、西裤加背心

● 单排扣和双排扣

单排扣：纽扣数量通常为一颗、两颗和三颗；

双排扣：纽扣数量通常为两颗、四颗和六颗。

相比之下，三件套更为传统，也更为正式。两颗扣（单排扣）西装和六颗扣（双排扣）西装为正统款，其余则为流行款。

西装款式的选择主要根据场合以及个人的身形和气质特点来决定，并不是越贵越合适，不应盲目追求名牌和潮流。

1.1.2 Shirt

Suits should be matched with suit shirts. The characters that differentiate a business shirt from a dress shirt or a casual shirt are as follows:

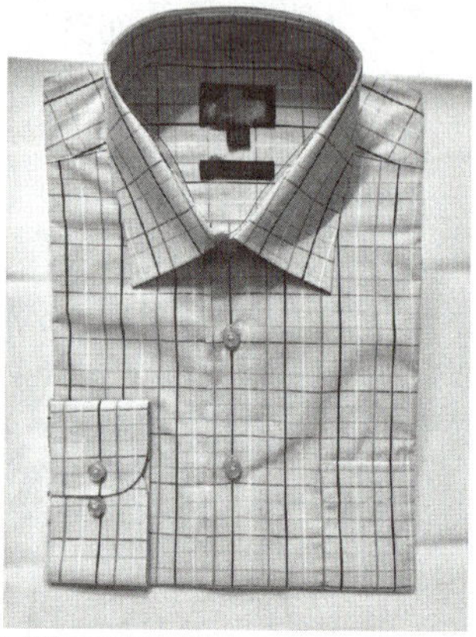

Texture: pure cotton or wool

Colors: solid in color (white as the first choice; sky-blue, gray, black second to it)

Collar: square collar as the best; short collar, long collar and button-down collar also preferred

Patterns: no patterns, white shirt with pinstripe also acceptable

Sleeves: long-sleeve

正装衬衫有别于礼服衬衫，没有礼服衬衫的繁复装饰，更适合以工作为主的职场，而非社交场合。

如果想营造一种法式优雅，法式衬衫（即双层袖口衬衫）是一个不错的选择，配以精致的袖扣，高品位的形象呼之欲出。

1.1.3 Tie

Tie is an indispensable part if you want to have your dress look formal enough for business occasion.

You should choose a tie in line with the suit, with solid color, or some patterns such as dots, pinstripes or plaid.

领带的打法

领带的打法多种多样，职场上比较常用的一般有平结、温莎结、半温莎结等。

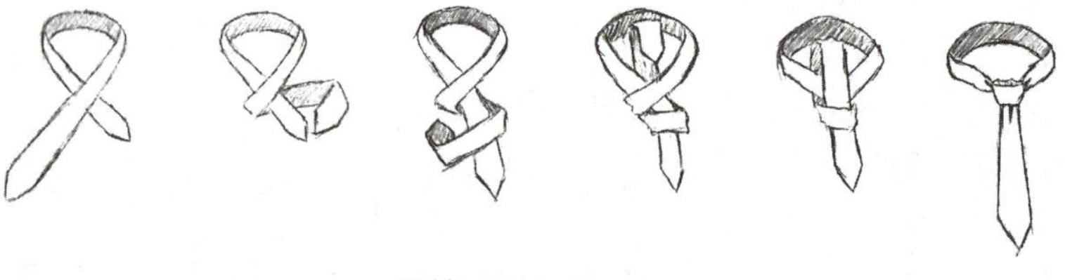

平结 (Plain Knot)

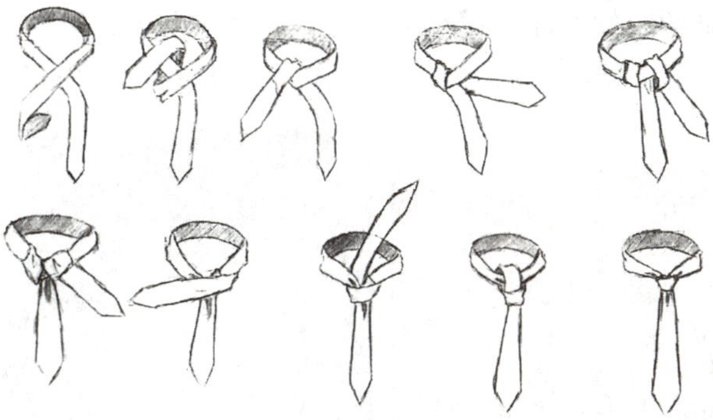

温莎结 **(The Windsor Knot)**

半温莎结 **(The Half-Windsor Knot)**

Case:

Joe is newly employed by a trade corporation and is going to work this morning. In order to be formal and professional, he dresses himself in gray business suit and chooses his favorite bow tie to go with it.

But when he arrives at the office, he finds that everybody frowns at him. Is there anything wrong?

1.1.4 Socks

西装皮鞋搭配的袜子要求为深色、单色款，最好是黑色。纯棉或纯毛的袜子是最好的选择，避免选择丝质或尼龙袜子。袜子要足够长，确保在坐下时不露出脚部皮肤。

1.1.5 Shoes

Leather shoes, especially cow leather shoes are preferred. According to conventions, businessmen should choose dark, solid-color leather shoes. Black leather shoes are a favorable choice as they match belts and briefcases easily. There are various styles of leather shoes. Oxfords and Derbies are suitable for suits.

在选择正装皮鞋的时候，注意避免镂空雕花、拼皮拼色、带有文字图案等装饰性强的款式。皮鞋的款式有多种，搭配正装的皮鞋往往为牛津鞋或者德比鞋。

区分牛津鞋和德比鞋：

牛津鞋：系带部分被鞋面压住，称为 closed lacing。

德比鞋：系带部分敞开（open lacing），鞋舌与鞋面连成一体。

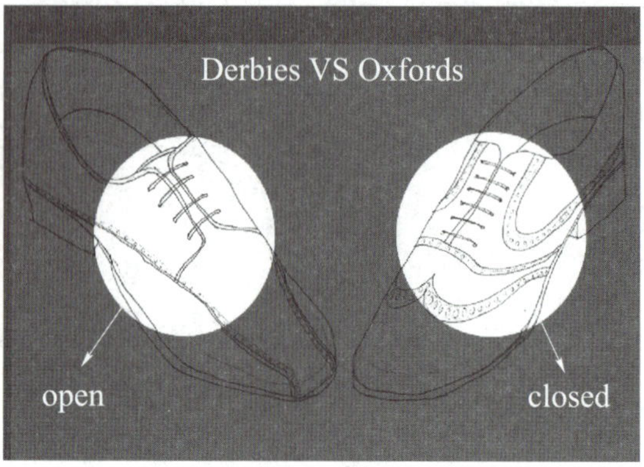

1.1.6 Belt

Belt is a necessity for businessmen. Leather belt is a good choice, as it is free from cracks and peeling due to the aging of PU. It would be better to choose a simple belt buckle with minimum decorations and avoid obvious logos of luxury.

1.1.7 Accessories

Compared with women's accessories, there is a less variety of accessories for men. The accessories that men wear include watches, rings, cufflinks and necktie bars (or tiepins).

Watch:

正装表，贵金属，手动，表径 36 mm～39 mm。

Ring:

佩戴数量不能超过一个，最好选择贵金属，造型稳重低调，镶嵌的宝石不显得夸张炫耀。

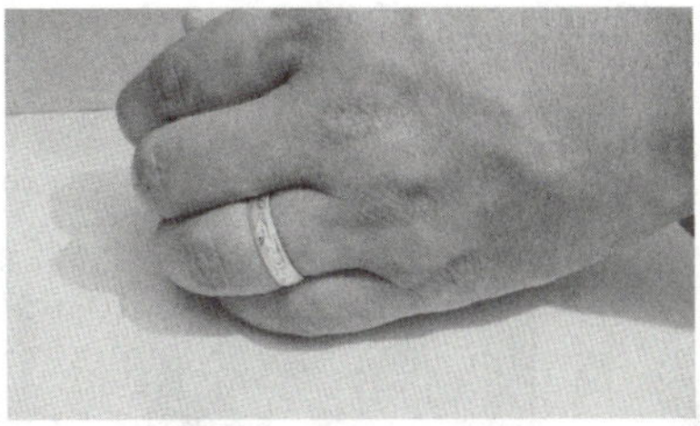

Cufflink:

袖扣须搭配法式衬衫。贵金属制成的袖扣加以钻石、宝石、珍珠等的装饰，让袖扣成为男士体现品位的重要职场配件之一。

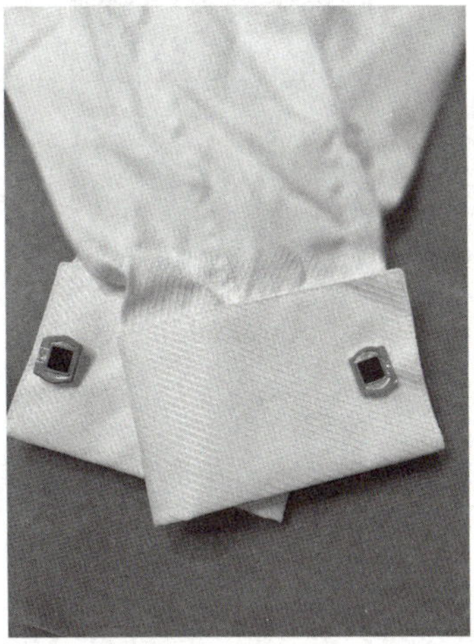

Necktie bar (or necktie pin):

领带夹可以起到固定领带的作用，一般置于领带的黄金分割点上，即衬衫从上往下第四至第五粒纽扣之间。但现在很多男士不使用领带夹，或是使用领带针。

Pocket square:

袋巾在旧时是用于掩盖鼻子以遮挡路上的灰尘和浊气，置于绅士们的胸袋中。随着纸巾的出现，袋巾渐渐没有了往日的功能，但一直没有被取代。颜色优雅、图案别致、材质上乘的袋巾在今天仍是品位和身份的象征。

Straight folding

Natural folding

Triangle folding

Briefcase:

一般建议选择真皮材质，深色单色，方形手提款式，能放下 A4 纸和文件袋的公文包。

1.2 Suggested items for keeping warm

In winter, men can put on a sweater and a coat so as to keep warm.

V neck sweater:

主要以羊毛、羊绒等保暖性好的面料为主。注意毛衣的数量不应超过一件，以免身形看起来臃肿。

Coat:

三款国际上常用于商务场合和社交场合的大衣外套：巴尔玛肯外套、柴斯特外套、波鲁外套。

Balmacaan **Chesterfield** **Polo**

2. Informal Business Dress

2.1 Dress

Blazer:

Blazer 最早产生于英国海军制服。严格地说，现代 Blazer 并不是一种西装上衣的名称，而是一种特定的搭配规则。

搭配的要求是：

上衣：海军蓝颜色面料、金属扣、戗驳领西装，有些款式胸前有徽章。

裤子：灰色或卡其色裤子。

Navy blue upper suit matching khaki pants

Jacket:

夹克风格比 Blazer 更为休闲，因此在面料、颜色和款式上要求比较少。职场上的夹克款式与西装相似，平驳领，棉麻、毛料、针织都可以，颜色种类多，无特别严格的搭配要求。

2.2 Shoes

Most casual shoes are made of leather but there are more choices.

Monk strap:

Monk strap 流行于鞋带出现之前。在现代，其正装鞋的地位已被系带款皮鞋取代。在相对休闲的场合，这款鞋还是热门之选。

Loafer：

Loafer 源于北美印第安人狩猎时穿的鹿皮软鞋（Moccasin）。这种鞋低帮、无鞋带，穿脱方便，穿着舒适，是非常受欢迎的休闲鞋款。光脚穿 Loafer 将其休闲的风格发挥到了极致，是潮人们的必备之选。而黑色的 Loafer 是众多 Loafer 中最正式的。

3. Social Dress

Businessmen will be in dress suit when attending social activities, because characters of dress suit are very different from that of suit worn on business occasions. The suit worn in workplace during the day is not suitable for social events at night; therefore, it is necessary for a businessman to prepare himself a dress suit.

男士的衣橱里除了工作时的着装，礼服也是很重要的部分。一个商务人士如果没有礼服，则会错过很多社交场合，错失与他人交流和扩大自己人脉圈子的好机会。

3.1　Formal social dress

Formal dress is considered as the most formal attire of all suits, and is suitable for very solemn and serious occasions.

Daytime (before 6:00 pm)	Morning coat
Night (after 6:00 pm)	Swallow-tailed coat (White Tie)

晨礼服（Morning Coat）是用于白天社交场合的最正式的礼服着装。它曾经是欧洲上流社会男士出席英国马场金杯赛穿着的服装，后来被应用于白天的庆典、教堂礼拜以及婚礼活动等场合。现代的商务领域也将其作为出席重要的日间社交活动的高规格礼服。

由于晨礼服是规格最高的日间社交服装，其搭配自然也是非常讲究的。

燕尾服（Swallow-Tailed Coat），在着装密码中常称为 White Tie，起源于十八世纪英国骑兵的服装造型。

燕尾服是最正式的晚间社交着装。

3.2 Semi-dress

Strictly regulated formal dress brings many inconveniences. With the development of business, businessmen attend various business events during the day, when the long tail of swallowtail causes them problems and embarrassment. At the beginning of the 20th century, the tuxedo and director's suit are the less formal replacement for the formal dress.

Daytime (before 6:00 pm)	Director's suit
Night (after 6:00 pm)	Tuxedo (Black Tie)

董事套装（Director's Suit）是日间的便礼服，与晨礼服的最大不同在于没有了长后摆。但其仍保留了礼服的一些特征。

塔士多礼服（Tuxedo）在着装密码中常被称为 Black Tie，在搭配上仍是以礼服的风格为主，尽管它是简化了的燕尾服。塔士多礼服是晚间的次正式礼服。

（青果领塔士多）

黑色上衣（缎面领，一粒扣）	黑色单侧章裤	黑色领结	白色翼领或企领礼服衬衫	黑色马甲（或黑色腰封）	黑色漆皮鞋

3.3 Common social dress

It is the simplest dress for social occasions, making it the lowest profile dress. Normal dress consists of black suit, white shirt and neck tie, and it is suitable for normal social activities.

4. Traditional Attire

4.1 Chinese tunic suit (Sun Yat-sen Jacket)

中山装（Chinese tunic suit）是以孙中山先生为名的一种，在广泛吸收欧美服饰的基础上，综合了日式学生服装（诘襟服）与中式服装的特点，设计出的一种立翻领有袋盖的四贴袋服装。

Chinese tunic suit, known as the Mao suit in Western countries, which is formal and internationally recognized as a Chinese style suit, can be worn on various formal occasions.

Wearing occasions:

1) important celebrations
2) solemn diplomatic occasions
3) important business conferences
4) annual meetings
5) places where one should show the image of China

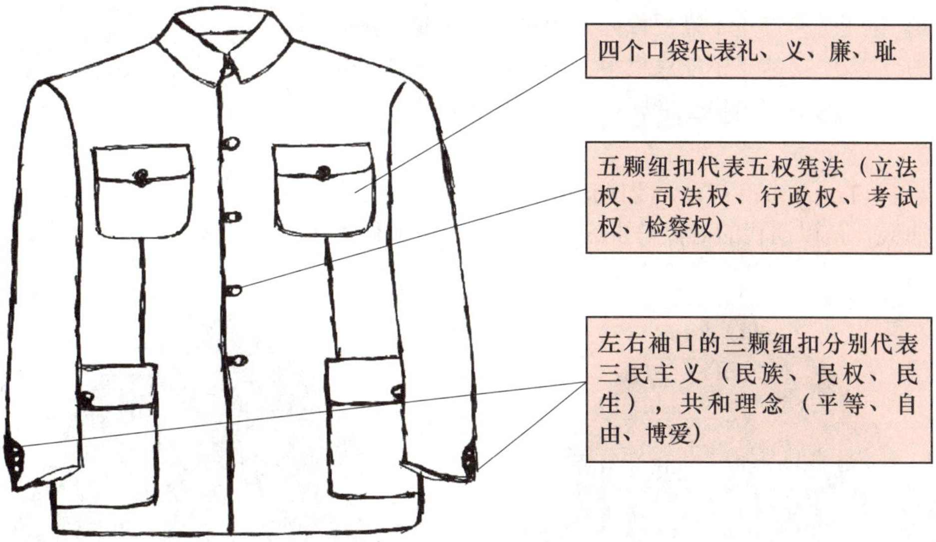

时代赋予中山装的政治含义

Chinese tunic suit is a clothing that embodies new ideas and concepts, which incorporates the concept of democracy and republic. It is the carrier of culture and etiquette, a sense of national pride as well.

随着时代的发展，中山装发展成两种风格，一种是标准版中山装，一种是改良版中山装。

标准版中山装

改良版中山装

The following points should be paid attention to when wearing Chinese tunic suit:

1) 穿之前必须熨烫，保持中山装的笔挺。
2) 穿着时必须扣好所有扣子，不可随意解开，更不要把对襟敞开。
3) 穿着时不要随意卷袖子。

4) 穿着时口袋里不需要像西装那样露出半截手帕。
5) 穿着时口袋里不能塞太多的东西以保持衣服平顺。
6) 穿着时最好内搭立领衬衫，搭配黑色皮鞋。

4.2 Tang suit (Tang Zhuang)

唐装，是以清代的对襟马褂为雏形，加入立领和西式立体裁剪所设计的现代服饰。

A Tang Suit (Tang Zhuang) is not a suit of the Tang Dynasty but a suit with Chinese style. Tang Suit are tailored according to specific procedures. Even the little buttons, which are the finishing touches of Tang Suit, are made with great detail. We should make brocade the first choice when selecting materials for Tang Suit. Symmetrical lapels and stand-up collars are typical styles. Exquisite embroidery is another feature of Tang Suit. Nowadays, absorbing some elements from Western designs, Tang Suit has a fashionable and beautiful look.

Wearing Tang Suit for formal occasions, such as attending celebrations, visiting other countries, attending conferences etc., is not only a fashion but also a reflection of cultural connotations, and a manifestation of national confidence.

Wearing suggestions:

1) 款式应选择如新唐装等经典款式。
2) 面料应选择织锦缎类等面料。
3) 唐装内可搭一件唐式衬衫，衬衫袖子不能外露。
4) 下身可穿搭小宽松西裤（注意：内搭衬衫下摆不要塞进裤腰内）。
5) 穿着时应把所有扣子系好。

Exercise 章节练习

1. Discussion

1) Please talk about your understanding of the saying "Apparel makes the man."

2) Yeda is a new employee and today is her first day in an insurance company. Are these dresses appropriate? Why or why not?

3) Scan the QR code to watch the video and discuss the following questions.

Q 1: From your perspective, which girl does a better job in matching her outfits and make-up?

Q 2: What are the relationships between make-up and cloth-matching? How do they affect each other?

4) Discuss the incident: A Dior's so-called hallmark Dior silhouette skirt has caused controversies lately. The skirt is a mid-length pleated skirt that has so many similarities to the Chinese traditional horse face skirt. (Read more about the incident through https://www.yicai.com/news/101476693.html.) Please talk about your understanding of the incident.

2. Case study

Referring to the principle of TPO and answer the question: Why are proper dresses so important?

Mr. Mo Yan's Swallow-tailed Coat

On November 10th, 2012, Chinese writer Mr. Mo Yan (莫言), dressed in a swallow-tailed coat, went up to the stage to receive his Noble Prize award in Stockholm, Sweden. Before Mr. Mo started his journey, heated discussion on the dress that Mr. Mo would choose was aroused.

Before the ceremony, Mo Yan's elder brother said "we have prepared a swallow-tailed coat", which caused the controversy in China. Some netizens figured that choosing the swallow-tailed coat is a phenomenon of "blindly worshiping foreign things", and wearing it indicates the trend to cater for Western culture, "it is neither fish nor flesh". Other netizens said, "Mo Yan, as a Chinese writer, abandoned the persistence of Eastern culture." Then, some netizens helped Mo Yan try on several dresses for award ceremony by Photoshop, including Chinese Hanfu (汉服), Tang suit (唐装), Chinese tunic suit (中山装) and Western business suit.

Why did Mo Yan choose swallow-tailed coat for Nobel Prize Award ceremony instead of the dresses recommended by Chinese netizens?

Please analyze the reasons from the perspective of dress code.

3. After-class activity (critical thinking)

At the 2001 Shanghai APEC Summit, heads of all states appeared in Tang attire. The 2014 Beijing APEC Summit leaders' clothing was a series of Chinese style clothing that showcased the new image of the Chinese people, known as the "New Chinese Clothing". Its root is "Chinese"; its soul is "Li", and its form is "New". "Zhong" represents China's tradition and civilization, "New" represents China's innovation based on inheritance and "Li" represents Chinese etiquette culture. In terms of style, it integrates classic Chinese styles from all ages.

Based on the attire of leaders from these two conferences, would you please talk about your understanding of cultural confidence and how is cultural confidence reflected in clothing?

Chapter Two

Grooming 仪表礼仪

学习任务

1. 了解职场中的发型要求。
2. 了解职场中女性的妆容特点及化妆技巧。
3. 了解职场中坐、站、行、蹲的基本仪态规则及标准。

Traditional thinking: Inner beauty is more important than the appearance.

Grooming: A Form of Hygiene

Case:

根据《华尔街邮报》(*Washington Post*)报道，迈阿密大学及经济学家迈克尔·弗兰奇(Michael French)做过一项调查：随机选择一组人，包括男性和女性，请他们对自己的外表做出评估，从"非常美丽或英俊"到"非常没有吸引力"分成五个等级，结果发现自认为外表美丽高于外表一般水平的女性，收入也相应地高出8%。这里的外表美丽，并不单只长得好看，更多倾向于对自己仪容仪表(grooming)的关注。

——《有礼行天下》(茱莉亚著)

Is it true that one more chance will be given to those who are considered to be more attractive? What are our standards of "attraction"? Here comes Chapter Two. Let's figure out the visible value of grooming.

—Background

Pay attention to the appearance. This is normally considered to be one of the many kinds of human beings' behavior. Do you know this behavior is not only applied to human, but also other species? Animals try to be more competitive in their own group by the means of combing furs and cleaning body.

According to Wikipedia, personal grooming (also called preening) is the art of cleaning, grooming, and maintaining parts of the body. It is a species-typical behavior. Many social animals adapt preening and grooming behaviors for other social purposes such as bonding and the strengthening of social structures. Grooming plays a particularly important role in forming social bonds in many primate species, such as chacma baboons and wedge-capped capuchins.

—Definition of grooming

Appearance:

Appearance basically refers to a person's look, which includes whether his/her features are in proportion, and how to balance looks, body shape with hair styles as well as clothing.

在中文中，我们用仪容仪表来表述相同的意思，就个人的整体形象而言，容貌是整个仪表中的一个重要环节，它反映一个人的精神面貌、朝气和活力，能传达给接触对象感官最直接、最生动的信息。本章内容主要包括容貌、身体和发型，还包括上一章所介绍过的服饰。

仪表不恰当的人，人们往往只看到其外在“不好”“不合适”的部分，而没有兴趣再进一步了解他/她的内涵。

Principles and basic requirements of women's grooming:

1) Elegant and in good taste

2) Clean and tidy

3) Simple and appropriate

Hair has proved its potential to make a statement as well as or more strongly than clothes do.

The amount of make-up sends an unavoidable message.

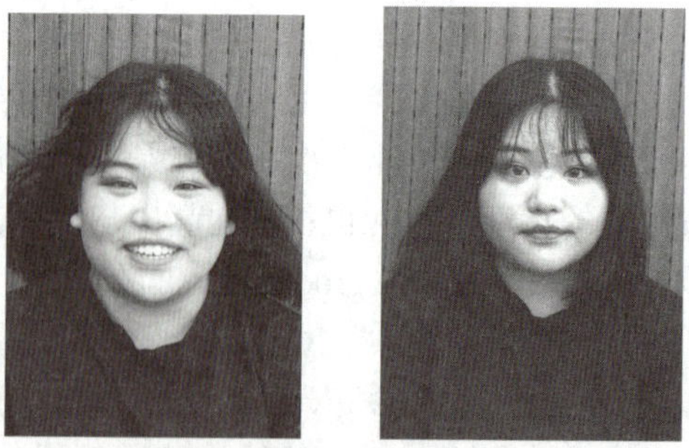

Sometimes, grooming can be your key.

I. Face 脸部

Contents:

1. Face cleansing
2. Rules in skin care
3. Tips for make-up

In our daily life, face can "speak" before you "talk". Therefore, keep it as clean and attractive as you can, since the point is to attract, not to repel.

1. Cleansing

我们经常听到一些女士苦恼甚至抱怨，我实在不懂化妆啊，不化妆不行吗？姑且不论化妆与否，保持面部干净清爽是第一步。所以，你需要了解正确的洗脸方法。

Cleansing removes make-up, dirt, and grease from the surface of the skin and is necessary for all skin types.

Steps of face-cleansing

1) Wash your face once or twice a day. If you have oily skin, please make sure you do it twice.
2) Use appropriate amount of facial cleansing milk/soap, etc. Make a circling movement gently on your face with your middle and ring fingers.
3) After cleansing, please do apply skin care products, which may basically include balancer, lotion, and cream.

2. Skin Care

2.1 Necessity

Skincare is one of the inevitable and basic needs of every woman. You can forget your make-up occasionally, but you never let go one single step of your skincare.

Reason No.1: Women are made up of water.

曹雪芹说过，女人是水做的骨肉。俗话也说，女人如水。这是指女人的眼泪，女人的眼睛，女人的话语，女人的情感，还有女人的皮肤。爱美首先体现在脸上，如何才能保持自信？首先得了解如何护肤。

Skincare is the range of practices that support skin integrity including nutrition, avoidance of excessive sun exposure and appropriate use of emollients, which enhances appearance. Skincare is a routine daily procedure in many settings. Our skin is the body's protective layer. It is not only defending against external bacteria, but also the measure standard of health and beauty.

Reason No. 2: Biologically speaking, women are more speedy in the aging process.

由于生理上的因素，女性衰老期衰老的现象比男性明显很多。医学研究表明，女性30 岁以后，部分女士是在生育之后，身体就因为雌激素水平的下降而慢慢衰老，皮肤各项指标也在下降，直接影响脸部的肤质。为了延缓衰老，保湿、紧致、抗皱就显得尤为重要。

2.2 Procedure

Basic steps of women' skincare process:

——日间护肤流程：

洗面奶

爽肤水

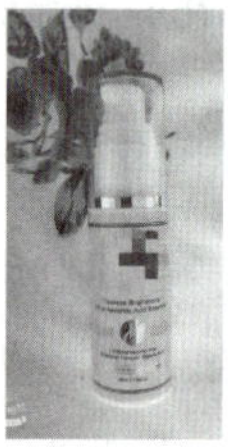

精华

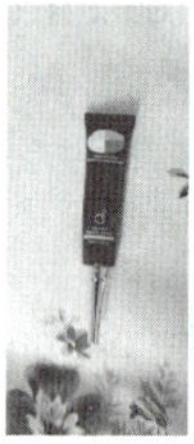

眼霜

乳液

面霜

隔离

——夜间护肤流程：

洗面奶

爽肤水

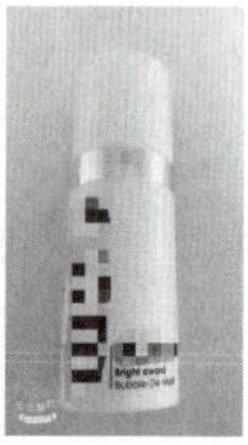

清洁滋养面膜

精华

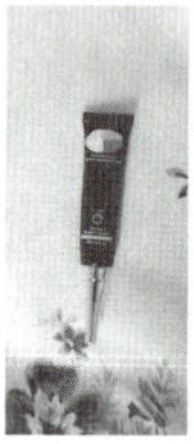

眼霜

乳液

面霜

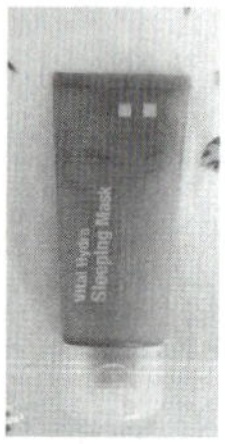

睡眠面膜

If you think it is too complicated:

Reduced Process:

— Cleansing
— Tonner/Balancer
— Lotion/Moisturizer
— Base/Color Correction Cream (CC)
— Sun Block

3. Make-up

Generally speaking, men do not wear make-up. Women, as a rule, or kind of international etiquette, use a light touch—however, make-up should enhance, not dominate.

一项英国科学家的研究表明：会化妆的女性平均收入往往高于不化妆的女性，而且显得更聪明。化妆其实不仅仅是一种自信的提升，同时也是对将要遇见的人的尊重。其次，做好化妆、卸妆的步骤不但不会为你的肌肤带来负担，而且还可以抵御紫外线、雾霾对肌肤所带来的伤害，简直是一举多得！

Whether you may have a perfect make-up basically depends on your achievements in skincare procedure. Make-up helps conceal or cover up those imperfections, like scars or acne.

Principles

- Light make-up
- Adopt good points and avoid shortcomings
- "3W" principles

WHEN/时间；WHERE/场合；WHAT/事情

3.1 Skin type

化妆会使皮肤变差这一说法早就站不住脚，皮肤保养更是男性和女性都应该关注的话题。选择合适自己的、质量过关的产品不但不会伤害皮肤，甚至可以达到保护真皮层，让你看起来容光焕发。首先，你需要了解自己的肤质。

皮肤类型 skin type

——油性皮肤：oily

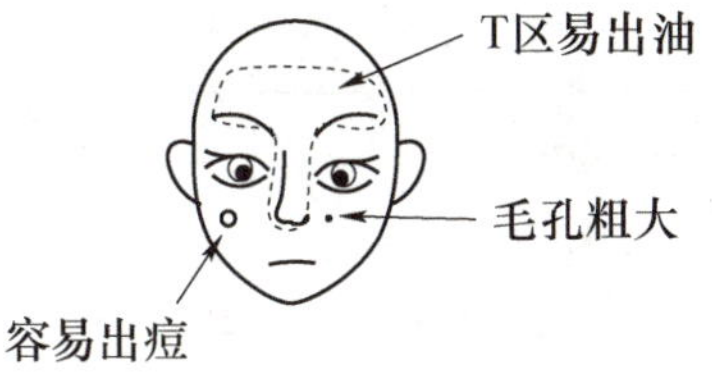

Tips：控油、补水、保湿

——干性皮肤：dry

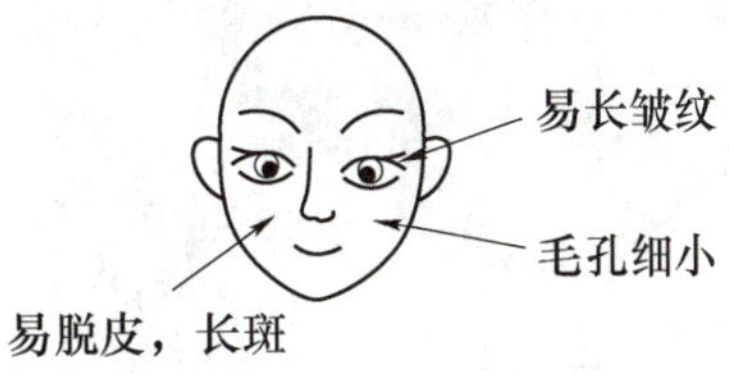

Tips：补水、保湿

——中性皮肤：neutral

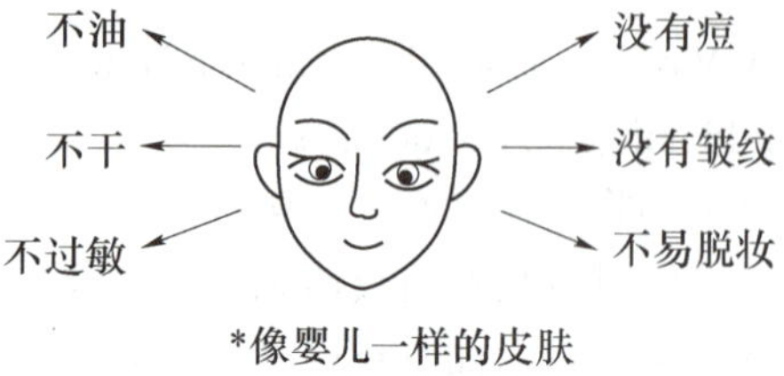

Tips：防止皮肤变干，要保湿！！

——混合性皮肤：combination

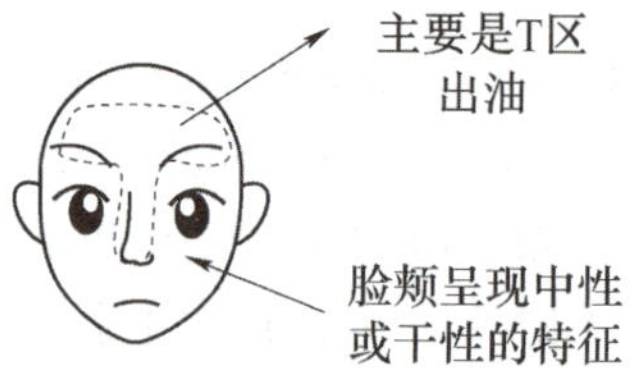

Tips：与油性皮肤区分开来！

——敏感性皮肤：sensitive

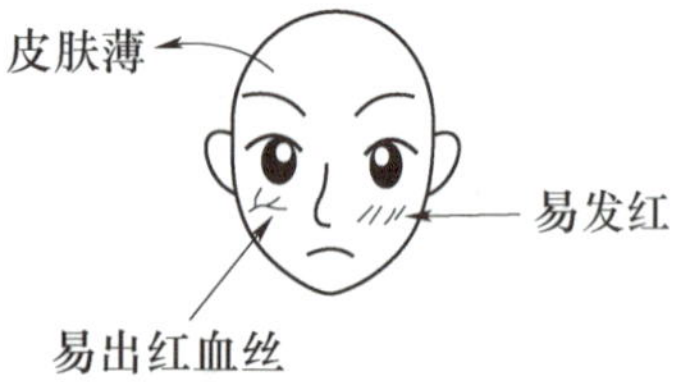

Tips：用柔和配方的产品护理

3.2 Type of products

彩妆 cosmetics

遮瑕膏：CONCEALER
修容饼：SHADING POWDER
粉底：FOUNDATION (COMPACT, STICK)
粉饼：PRESSED POWDER
闪粉：SHIMMERING POWDER/GLITTER

眉粉：BROW POWDER
眉笔：BROW PENCIL
眼线液（眼线笔）：LIQUID EYELINER
眼影：EYE SHADOW
睫毛膏：MASCARA

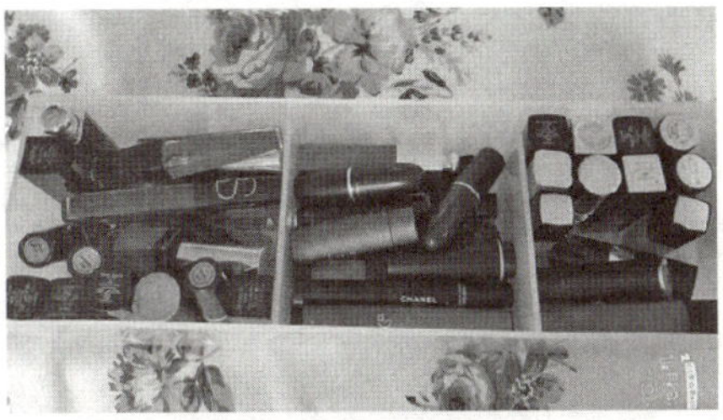

唇线笔：LIP LINER
唇膏：LIP COVER/LIPSTICK
唇彩：LIP GLOSS/LIP COLOR

腮红：BLUSH
卸妆水：MAKE-UP REMOVER

3.3　Procedure

Procedures of daily business makeup：

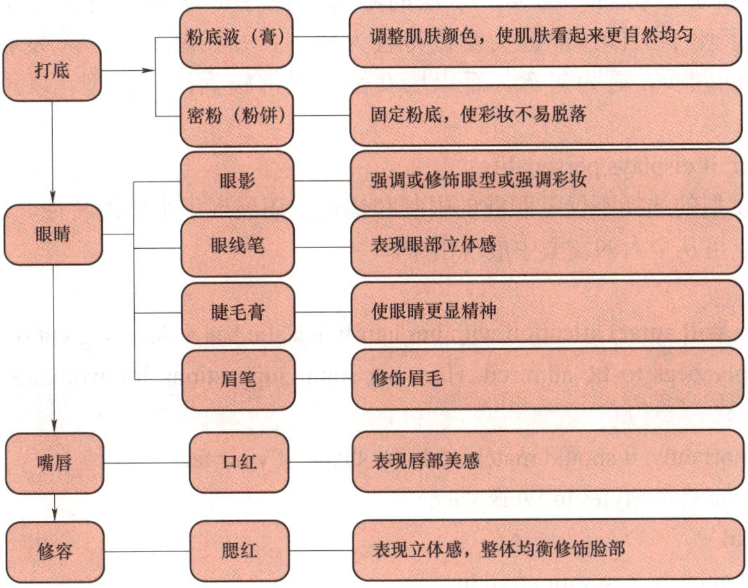

再补充两点，请注意：

1)“个人专用”原则——不可随意使用他人化妆品；

2)“补妆、化妆回避”原则——不在公共场合化妆和补妆，不以残妆示人。

Attention:

Taboos of make-up in business occasion:

1) "Heavy" lower lash liner

2) Overuse of brush

3) Dark smoky eyes and the Cat's eye make-up

4) Too pinky make-up

5) Dark color lip

II. Hair 发型

Contents:

1. Appropriate hair styles in work places
2. Hair tidiness

Hairstyle is a crucial component of human being's appearance; you can show your characteristics in different hairstyles.

Initially, a hairstyle shows your occupation and social class.

从古至今，人们对发型的要求就跟着装一样。古时候，发型甚至标志着人们的社会地位和阶级属性。现今，职业的不同也往往可以从发型上表现出来，如护士、空姐为了便于工作，常将头发梳得较为整齐，并在脑后扎一个发髻；学生在发型方面的限制较少，更为随意，而职场女性则通常较为注重发型，以求体现其专业的一面。

Moreover, it displays personality.

其实，发型的选择不仅是职业的限制和体现，还展现了个体的特性。活泼开朗、大方知性等特点可从个人的发型中展现出来。

A woman will attract attention with her hair when she has a flattering cut or healthy, shiny hair that simply begs to be admired. Here are some suggestions for women's hair styles in workplaces:

Most importantly, it should match with the shape of your face.

Appropriate Hair Styles in Workplace:

- Ponytail
- Short but curly, wavy, or straight
- Tuck it behind ears
- Pull it out with a barrette

Oval Square Round Oblong Heart

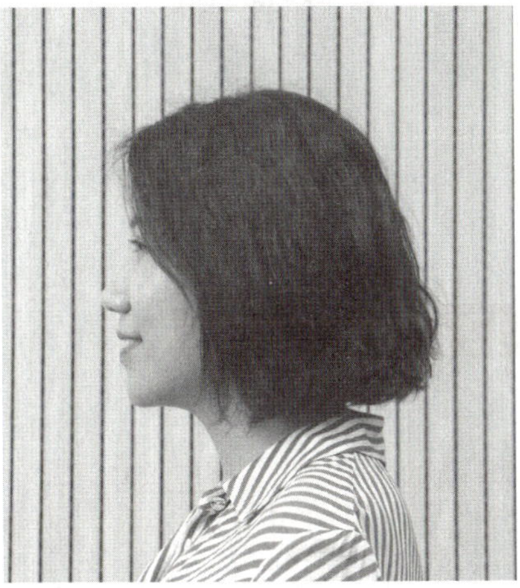

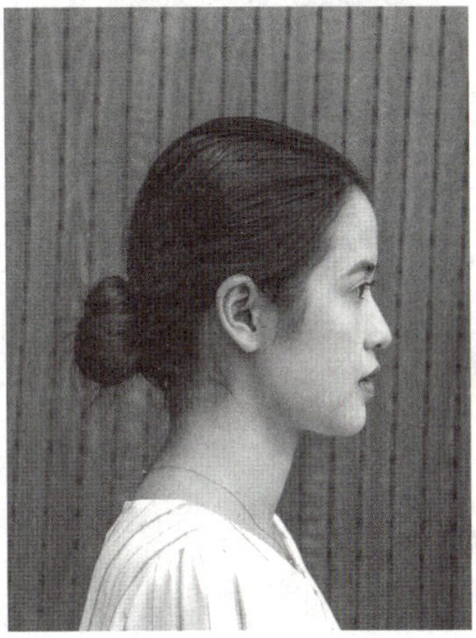

Attention! No matter what kind of hair style you choose, KEEP IT CLEAN!

注意：为了保持蓬松和干净，一般 1～2 天要清洗一次头发。特别是在重要的约会或者会面之前，清洗头发，去除头屑和异味是十分有必要的。头皮屑和油腻的头发会影响人与人之间的交往。同时，洗发可以使头发蓬松，从而提升面部肤色的亮度，使人看起来更有神采。

III. Hands 手部

Contents:

Important points in hand and nail care

人们常说，手是女人的第二张脸，手部的护理是女人形象的重要部分，同时还可以展现个人的修养和气质。手部保养一般包括：手部皮肤的干净、滋润；手掌、手指的柔软灵活；指甲的保护与修饰。需要重点关注的是指甲的清洁。

Nails should be kept clean and trimmed. Keep a nail clipper in your desk drawer; while trimming the fingernails, push back the cuticles occasionally.

The best length of women's nails: over the tip of the finger

Preferable nail color: light or transparent

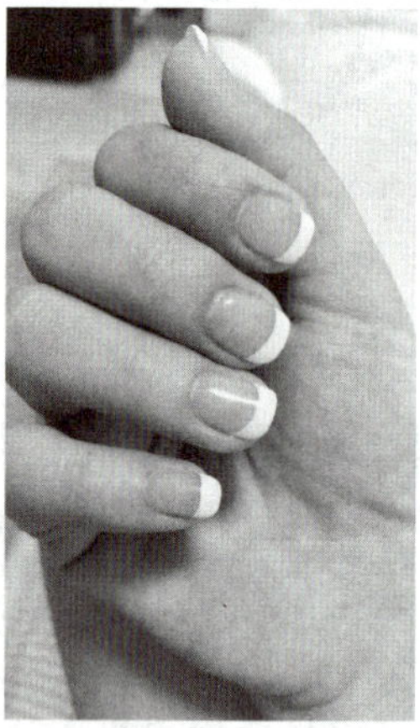 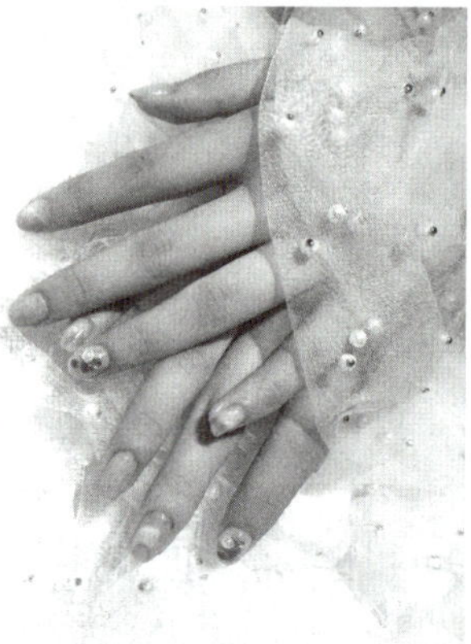

IV. Oral Hygiene and Body Odor 口腔卫生和体味

Contents:

1. Oral hygiene
2. Body odor

1. Oral Hygiene

现今，求职者们在过五关斩六将的过程中越来越体会到“高颜值”的重要性。诚然，良好的外形条件确实可以在面试时为你挣得一席之地。然而，除上面提到的着装、妆容外，求职者们往往会忽略一个关键细节：牙齿。

职场中，满口蛀牙或者一口黄牙，再加上交谈中难闻的口气，摆在你面前即使有再多的机会都会溜走。据统计，在招聘会上，因形象问题被拒的求职者达到 30%～40%，这其中因为牙齿引出的问题不在少数。

Suggestions:

1) Brush your teeth daily for more than once.
2) Less food with pungent smell.
3) Prepare chewing gums, dental floss and breath mint if necessary.
4) Visit the dentist for professional tooth wash occasionally.

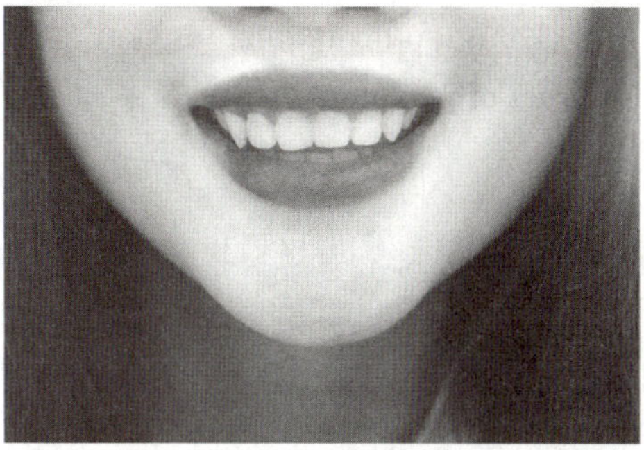

2. Body Odor

体味是职场中不得不面对的一个非常重要的问题。有些人因为身体的因素导致有让人掩鼻的汗味或者体味，如狐臭；有些人为了掩盖自身的某些味道而喷洒浓重的香水，让人窒息，其所过之处甚至有杀虫水的味道。

So, here are the tips if you do not know how to deal with problems of body odor:

1) Do not use too much perfume. Make sure the scent is light and clean.

2) A daily shower is the best defense against body odor, or body deodorant is quite advisable and useful.

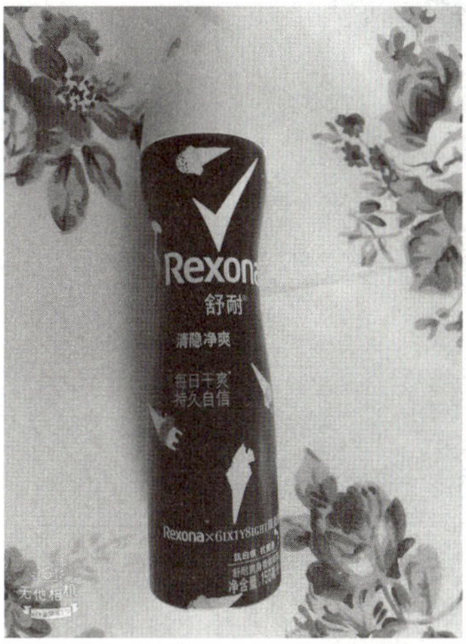

Background information of perfume

—Types of perfume

Perfume (Parfum)

香精perfume（Parfum）

浓度在20%以上，香味持续力约为6～8小时。

Eau de Parfum (EDP)

香水（Eau de Parfum）

香精浓度约在15%～20%之间，价格属中等价位，比较大众化，被广泛使用，所以才会以香水代称所有的香水种类，而不是香精。持续力约4小时左右，通常简称为E.D.P.。

Eau de Toilette (EDT)

淡香水（Eau de Toilette）

浓度约在5%～15%之间，因此价格最便宜，不过持续力最差，大约只有2～3小时，多使用于沐浴之后。从这个等级开始才有较多的男性香水。

Eau de Cologne(EDC)

古龙水（Eau de Cologne）

它是男性香水的一般等级，至于女性香水在这个阶段已经很少见了。古龙水的浓度只有2%～4%，香味持续力约只有一两个小时。

Eau Fraiche

清香水（Eau Fraiche）

香精含量非常低，只有1%～2%，似乎已经不被划归在香水的范围内，上市的体香剂、须后水都属于这个等级，香味的持续力非常短。

The note of perfume

一般来说，一种良好品质的香水均具有三段式香味，由前调、中调、后调表现出起承转合的韵律感。

将香水涂抹在手腕、颈部、耳后、臂弯里等有脉搏跳动的部位，这样香味随着脉搏跳动、肢体转动而飘溢散发；也可将香水喷洒于腰部、髋关节，这是为了让余香更持久；脚踝处也可喷洒香水，这样可使香味飘散更自然。女士还可在裙裾处洒少量香水，随着身体走动，散发香味。

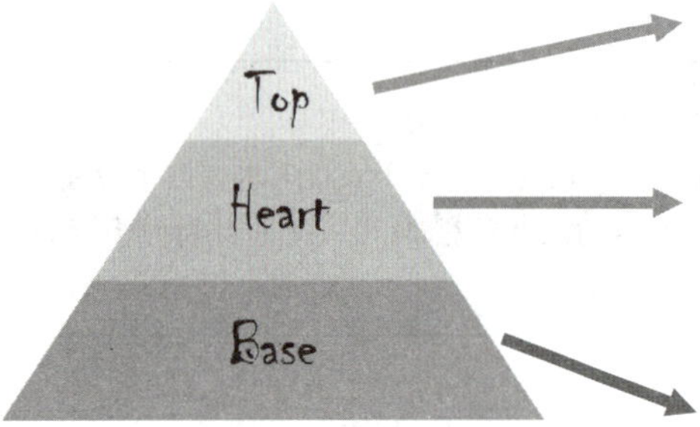

Top Note（前调）

最开始香水喷后的轻淡香味，持续8～15分钟左右。

Heart/Middle Note（中调）

此时的香味是香水主要的味道，通常在香水喷后30分钟，在前调散去之后而来，持续10分钟左右。

Base Note（后调）

香水喷后约30分钟后才会有的香味，是表现个性最好的香味。这种香味是香水味混合个人肌肤以及体味所产生的综合味道。

V. Manners 仪态

Contents:

1. Manners in sitting
2. Manners in standing
3. Manners in walking
4. Manners in squatting

Warm-up:

Under what circumstances will these posture positions be seen?

1. Manners in Sitting

An old saying goes: A proper sitting position is required when sitting. A proper sitting position gives people around an impression of elegance, seriousness, and balance. What's more, it shows a person's internal cultivation and spiritual outlook. Those who sit too unbendingly, especially women, will leave a bad taste in the mouth, and be considered vulgar and rude.

无论男女，在正式场合就座时请做到：

1) 椅子两侧都无障碍物时，从椅子后方的左侧入座。

2) 就座时只坐满椅子的 2/3，沙发的 1/2。

3) 落座时动作要轻，尽量不发出声响。

1.1 Women's manners in sitting

Women's sitting position is limited by their dress. Therefore, they adjust their body movement mainly by changing the positions of their calves. But no matter what position you choose, never forget to sit upright with back erected, knees together, and hands easily on your lab.

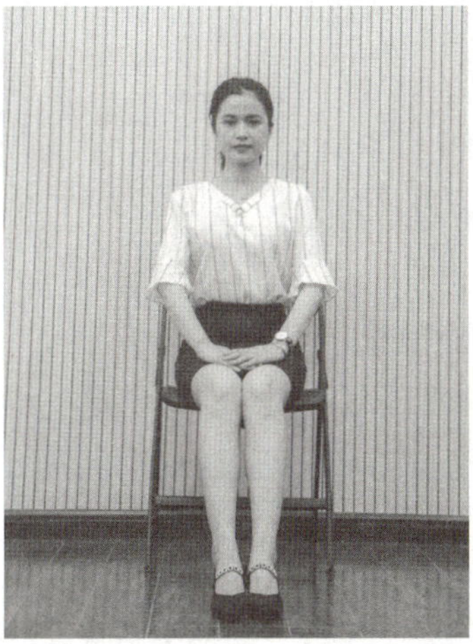

自然坐姿：双腿并拢，垂直于地面

斜放式坐姿：双腿并拢，同时向左或右倾斜

前后式坐姿：双膝并拢，双脚前后放置

叠放式坐姿：双膝并拢，小腿前后交叉叠放在一起

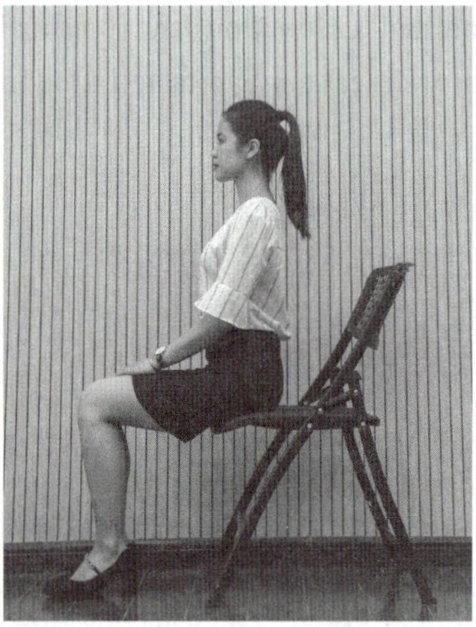

侧面：脖子、背、腰呈直线

女性在落座和就座时还应牢记：

1) 坐下之前先将裙子捋平。
2) 双膝始终并拢。
3) 不要不停摆弄头发、衣服、饰物等东西。
4) 手提包应放地上，而不是椅子上，更不能抱着。
5) 落座时动作要轻，尽量不发出声响。

1.2 Men's manners in sitting

The placement of knees: men usually keep their knees shoulder-width apart when sitting.

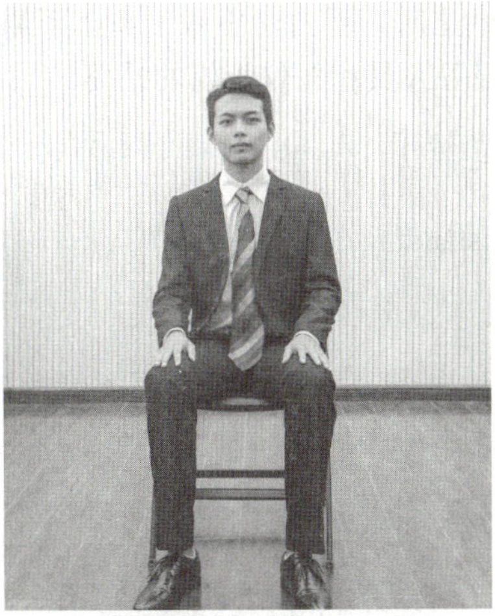

自然坐姿：双膝打开，与肩同宽

叠腿坐姿

2. Manners in Standing

Standing, just as sitting, is a static posture. Standing beautifully shows a fit body shape, graceful poise, as well as internal cultivation.

2.1 Women's manners in standing

When standing, it is advisable for women to keep knees together, shoulders pulling back a little bit, chest up and suck in the stomach.

标准式站姿：脚尖并拢，双手自然下垂于身体两侧

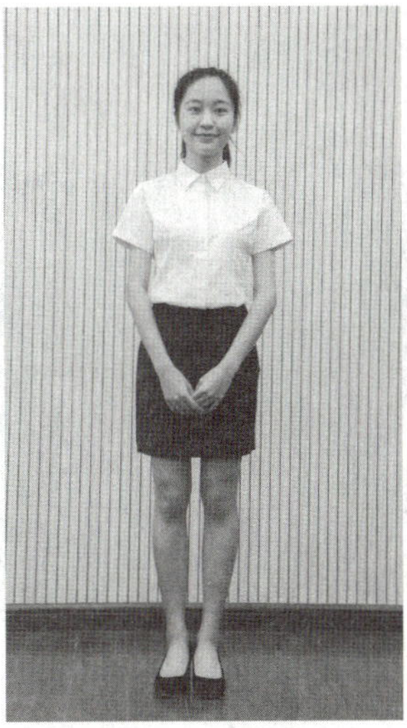

自然式站姿：脚跟并拢，脚尖稍向外打开，双手自然下垂于前腹处交叠

丁字步站姿：双脚前后站立，前脚跟置于后脚窝处，脚尖向外呈 30°

在日常的商务交往或社交活动中，女性在站立时，手自然下垂于身体两侧或自然下垂于前腹处交叠，而双手置于腰际处交叠则是服务人员和礼仪小姐的站姿。

2.2 Men's manners in standing

Men keep knees either closed or opened when standing.

标准站姿：双腿并拢，
双手自然下垂于身体两侧

自然站姿：双腿打开同肩宽，
双手自然下垂于身前交叠

像他们这样站：

3. Manners in Walking

Walking is a dynamic movement and a body language in business situation. People look fresh and confident with proper behaviors in walking.

注意：
1) 行走时上身挺直、双肩齐平，提气收腹，挺胸立腰。
2) 步速均匀。
3) 避免穿鞋跟有金属片的鞋子，以免发出过大的响声。

3.1 Basic concept of walking manner

Walking manner is the presence that a person shows when walking. A good walking manner is the reflection of dynamic beauty. A proper and graceful walking manner can make the walker look confident, elegant and cultured. Therefore, a proper walking manner is the most basic and essential etiquette in walking.

3.2 Self-discipline in walking

No eating, smoking, spitting or dropping litter while walking.

边走边吃或抽烟、随地吐痰或乱扔垃圾是进行礼仪的大忌，尤其是商务场合的绝对禁忌。

No cuddling or excessive intimacy.

行进时搂搂抱抱、勾肩搭背或过分亲昵，都是不符合行进礼仪要求的，商务场合更是要注意举止分寸。

Obey the traffic rules.

遵守交通规则是行进时的最基本最重要的准则，过马路看红绿灯、根据路标指示行进等任何时候都必须遵照执行。

3.3 Meeting someone when walking

When meeting an acquaintance in walking, you should greet him or her properly in about a meter away, by saying hi or waving hands; for strangers, if the distance is very close between two people for the sake of narrow roads or limited space, you should just nod your head to him or her. If the passageway is too narrow to pass for two persons, one should stop and let the other go first; if the other person also stops, you could go first and should say thanks.

3.4 Women's manners in walking

To show elegance, women should not walk too fast but with a shorter stride of 20 centimeters. Place one foot in line with the other. Otherwise, the image will be severely damaged. Keep hands waving naturally and body balanced.

3.5 Men's manners in walking

Men should avoid walking with parallel movement. Walk with toes forward and out a little bit, but not too much.

像他们这样走：

4. Manners in Squatting

Squat is a dynamic gesture. People need to squat or bend down in order to pick up things. Although people do not squat as frequently as they walk or stand, neglecting proper manners in squatting will damage one's elegant image.

注意：

1) 下蹲时臀部不能向后翘起，不能高于肩部。
2) 下蹲时应采用屈腿式蹲姿。
3) 下蹲时双腿不能叉开。
4) 必要时，女士在下蹲的同时用手稍微遮挡前胸处。

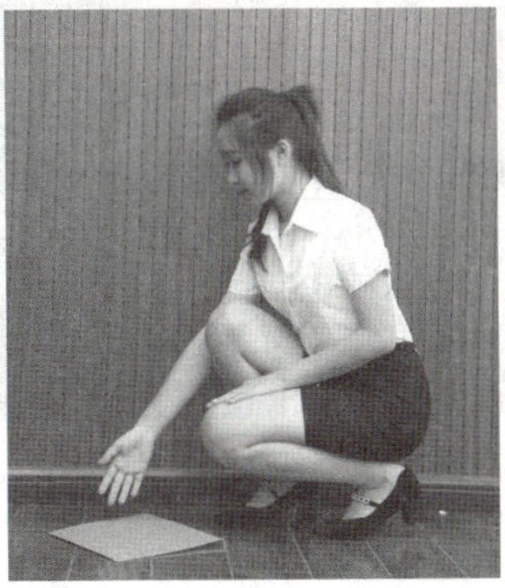

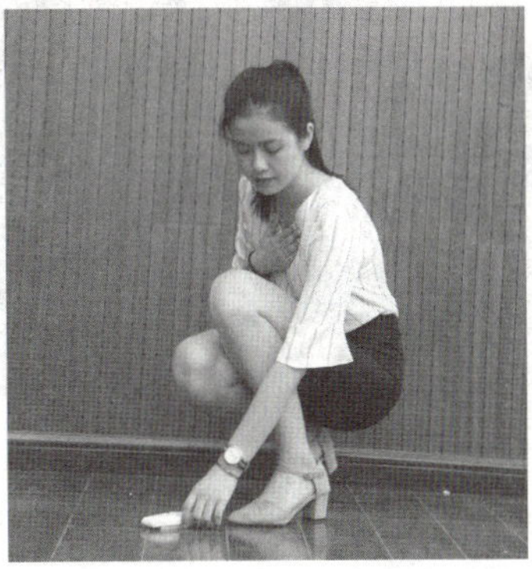

Exercise 章节练习

1.Classify the following pictures into "Dos" and "Don'ts" on business occasions.

A

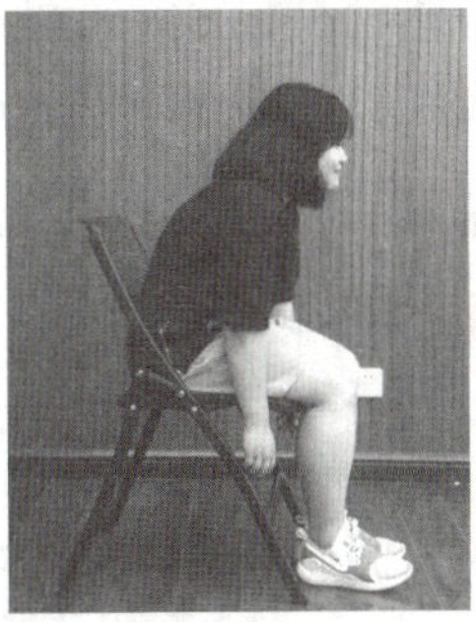

B

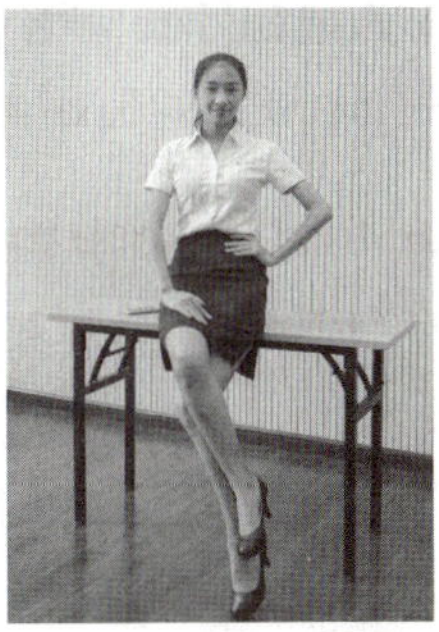

C

D

E

F

G

H

I

2. Tutorial

(Theme) Make-up and different occasions:

Please divide the class into groups, and give them 30-40 minutes to finish their make-ups according to the following requirements and circumstances.

A. Daily office occasion

B. An evening dinner party (black tie)

C. Negotiation conference with customers from Arabic countries.

D. Formal date with your fiancé/fiancée and his/her parents.

E. In ASEAN Expo, acting as a liaison officer/interpreter for a representative of foreign enterprise.

3. Scan the QR code to watch the video clip and try to notice what the wrong doings are in attire and grooming.

Module Three

Etiquette in Business Contact

交往礼仪

Chapter One Etiquette in Greeting 见面礼仪

学习任务

1. 了解职场中见面时问候的不同方式。
2. 了解名片上的必要信息以及交换名片时应遵循的礼仪。
3. 了解受礼、回赠礼、拒礼的礼仪，以及具有中国文化特色的商务赠礼佳品。
4. 了解赠礼礼仪的一些中英文化差异和其他国家的赠礼习俗。

I. Greeting 问候

Contents:

Different ways of greeting

Warm-up:

How do they greet each other in the following pictures? Do you know some other ways of greeting?

There are various ways of greeting in business occasions. A proper greeting in accordance with the occasions and cultures is a basic etiquette for businessmen. A good knowledge of greeting rituals helps to reduce the negative impacts of culture shock.

1. Handshake

Handshake is the most common way of greeting in international business situations.

1.1 Principles in handshaking

Intention of Handshaking: it is up to the top executives, the senior managers and ladies to decide whether to shake hands or not. That is to say, supervisors, the senior managers and ladies can extend their hands first.

However, on the occasion where a person holds two or three corporate positions, there may be problems in deciding who should be the first to extend their hand. For example, an ordinary female employee meets a top male executive, who should be the first to extend their hand?

People can follow TPO principle to decide who initiates the handshake in different occasions.

—Business occasion: hierarchy is the most important principle.

—Social occasion: age and gender are priorities.

1.2 Manners in handshaking

1) Extend the right hand in most occasions.

2) Hats and gloves should be taken off. (Soldiers, ladies with gown and long gloves are exceptions.)

3) Last 3-5 seconds.

4) Don’t squeeze but shake firmly.

5) Make eye contact.

6) Keep your hands clean.

握手礼源于原始社会，在狩猎时，人们手上经常拿着石块或者棍棒作为防御武器。他们遇到素不相识的人时，如果大家都无敌意，就要放下手上的东西并伸开手掌让对方摸摸手心以示友好。随着时代的变迁，这种习惯逐渐演变成握手礼。握手是我们日常生活中最普遍的一种礼节。

2. Hug

Hugging is also a common way of greeting in international business communication.

拥抱礼最早起源于交战双方和谈见面时，互相拥抱向对方保证没有暗藏武器。这种习惯慢慢演变成表达尊重、真诚和关爱的礼仪了。

但是，由于拥抱礼身体接触较多，并非人人适用。因此，在商务场合中必须根据与对方的关系以及对方的文化风俗来判断是否适合行拥抱礼。

2.1 Depending on the relationship

Generally speaking, hugging between close friends or families does not make people awkward, but it is offensive to hug a person who is not so close to you or whom you meet the first time.

2.2 Depending on the cultural customs

Cultures that accept hugging: the US, Mexico, Australia, France, Russia, etc.

Cultures that reject hugging: China, India, Japan, the Republic of Korea.

3. Bisou

Bisou is popular in Europe, especially in France.

Note 1: Bisou is barely touching the cheek, or just air kiss.

Note 2: In business situations, bisou is a way of greeting between two people who are close to each other. In most cases, men and women or women and women do cheek kiss.

如果用嘴唇行贴面礼，会被认为粗鲁甚至不雅。更为难堪的是，如果嘴唇不够干净，会让对方感觉到不舒服。

Note 3: Begin with the right cheek and repeat cheek kisses 2 to 3 times. Saying “mua” is acceptable if you know the person well.

4. Baisemain

Baisemain originates from the Vikings’ customs of “handing out gifts” to the king. Then it became popular in European and Latin American countries.

吻手礼是西方礼仪文化的一种传承。

达·芬奇在画作《丽达与天鹅》中，讲述了宙斯爱上了埃托利亚国王的女儿丽达，便化作天鹅与她见面。行吻手礼时，女生伸出来的手很像天鹅优雅的姿态。

Note 1: Men and women kiss hands, but it seldom happens between people of the same sex.

Note 2: Baisemain should be given to married women.

Note 3: Men should hold the women's hand with both hands, lower his head and then kiss lightly on her hand bump.

5. Bow

Bowing is popular in Eastern countries, such as Japan, Thailand, the Republic of Korea and the Democratic People's Republic of Korea. Executed standing or kneeling, bowing is an act to show one's greeting or respect to the seniors, the peers or the customers. Though it originated from China, bowing is more fastidious in modern Japan, the Democratic People's Republic of Korea and the Republic of Korea.

In the business intercourse nowadays, bowing is widely used in social occasions, especially in the service industry.

鞠躬礼起源于中国，是商代的一种祭祀的仪式。将祭品牲畜的肉切成块后卷起成圆形，以表达祭祀者对上天的崇敬。

鞠躬礼一直沿袭到现代，人们用这种方式来表达对地位尊者和长辈的问候或敬意。

行鞠躬礼时应该做到：

1) 行礼前先脱帽。

2) 站立，双手下垂于身体两侧。女性行鞠躬礼时，双手通常交叠置于身前。

3) 以腰部为轴心，上身前倾。

4) 面带微笑，同时致问候语。

Different degrees of lowness of the bow are regarded as appropriate for different circumstances.

- A bow at 15 degree is used in the business or social occasions to show greeting or warm welcome.
- A bow at 30 degree is to the seniors or the customers to show thanks or respect.
- A bow at 45-90 degree is considered deeper than the previous ones. It is usually used to show one's sincere apology and therefore it asks for a careful use.

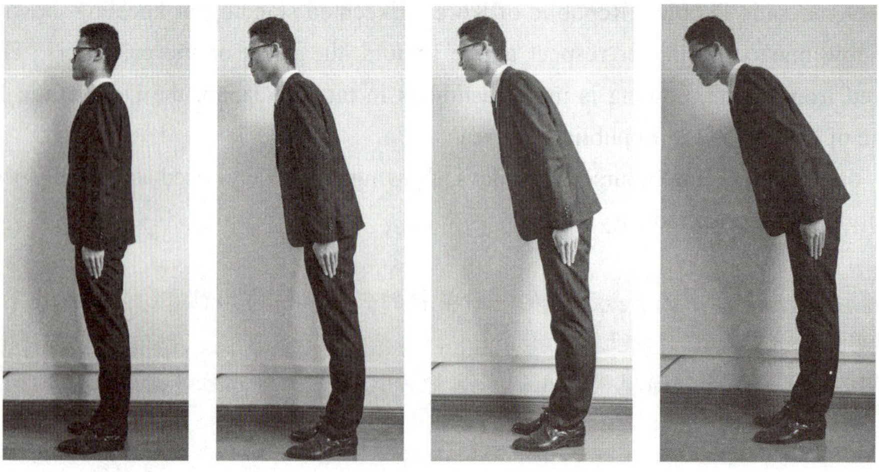

在中国：
15 度的鞠躬礼也称为草礼，是用于迎接客户的致意式礼仪。
30 度的鞠躬礼称为章礼，是用于感谢或恭送客户的致谢式礼仪。
45 度～90 度的鞠躬礼称为楷礼，是用于向客户道歉的致歉式礼仪。

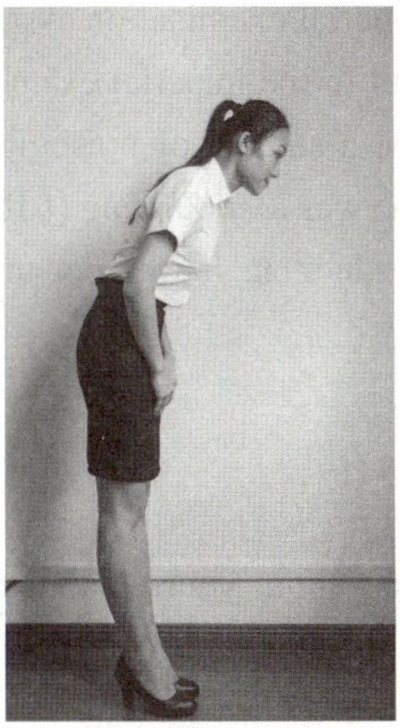

迎接客户时，
15 度致意式鞠躬

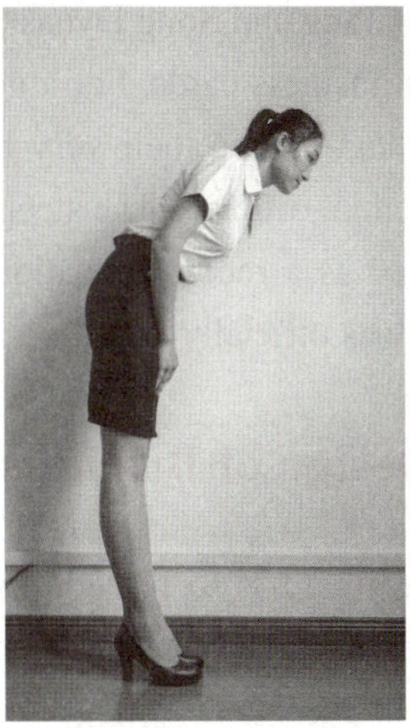

感谢或恭送客户时，
30 度致谢式鞠躬

向客户表示歉意时，
90 度致歉式鞠躬

II. Exchanging Business Cards 交换名片

Contents:

1. The origin of business cards
2. The design of business cards
3. Etiquette in exchanging business cards

Warm-up:

Case

Allen is a manager's assistant. On a business banquet, the manager introduced him to the CEO. After greeting each other, Allen reached into the patch pocket for his business card, and handed it to the CEO with the utmost respect. But the CEO showed an unpleasant face, and the conversation ceased. Allen was confused and wondered why the CEO who was initially kind and friendly changed his attitude quickly. What is your opinion?

In the business communication, people exchange cards at the first meeting, which helps to establish business contact and shows respect and self-cultivation to each other.

1. The Origin of Business Cards

Business cards had a history with more than 2,000 years in China. They were firstly made of bamboo or pieces of wood, called *Ye* (谒) in Qin Dynasty when the emperors used them before the meeting for a strategic partnership. At the end of Eastern Han, *Ye* was renamed *La* (刺) which was made of paper. In Tang and Song Dynasty, the imperial examination system had contributed to the population of business cards. For a good result in the imperial exam so as to launch a political career, candidates tried their very best to be a student of prestigious teachers and to be a disciple of influential officials. The stepping stone was *Men Zhuang* (门状) or *Ming Tie* (名帖) which functioned as a recommendation or introduction. It was not until Qing Dynasty that the business card was officially called.

2. The Design of Business Cards

The main function of a business card is to provide information about yourself and the company. An informative and well-designed business card impresses people most. The information on business card includes:

1) Name of the company/organization

2) Name of the individual

3) Title of the individual

4) Logo of the company/organization

5) Means of contact (address, phone number, fax number, mobile phone number, Email address…)

The printed business card should be kept in a wallet or a business card case rather than a pocket in case they get folded. Prepare sufficient business cards before you go to work.

注意：

- 地址应该写得尽量详细，提供门牌号码、道路、城区、城市、省（区）、国家的名称，以及邮政编码。
- 电话号码、传真号码应在前面加上国家的国际代码。
- 注意版面颜色的搭配，忌讳使用红色书写人名。
- 如有需要，可以在名片上加上公司的经营范围或公司简介等信息。
- 如果公司主要从事对外贸易，最好准备不同语言翻译版本的名片。

3. Etiquette in Exchanging Business Cards

Generally speaking, business cards should be exchanged before an activity or meeting, so that people can get the information as early as possible, and it also shows your respect to the person. When exchanging business cards, mind the following tips:

—Stand up.

—Shake hands before exchanging business cards. In some countries, such as China, people hold two corners of the card with both hands, and present the card with the print facing up so that it can be easily read.

—Smile and make eye contact.

—Say something nice, such as "nice to meet you" "keep in touch".

—After receiving the card, read the information on the card carefully before you put the card in the wallet or card case. Do not just put the card aside or put into your pocket immediately.

—Try to remember the name on the card, if you have questions, ask directly.

注意：

各国在交换名片时遵守不一样的礼仪，并非所有国家都遵循相同的规则。

- 印度、中东地区和一些东南亚国家（如印度尼西亚、马来西亚、柬埔寨）忌讳用左手传递物品。因此交换名片时常常只使用右手。
- 英国人认为交换名片可以不需要过于严肃，有时候即使把名片放进口袋也可以接受。
- 注意不同英语国家对同样的头衔表述有一定的差别，如英国人说"Chairman"，而美国人习惯用"President"。

III. Etiquette in Gifting 赠礼礼仪

Contents:

1. Etiquette in receiving, giving and refusing gifts in China
2. Different customs of gifting between China and other countries
3. Gifts in business with China's unique culture
4. Gifting etiquette in other countries

Warm-up:

1. What is the etiquette in receiving gifts?
2. What kind of gifts do you think are not acceptable? How to refuse them?

1. Etiquette in Receiving, Giving and Refusing Gifts in China

1.1 Etiquette in receiving gifts

Receiving gifts in the business world should be paid attention to some details.

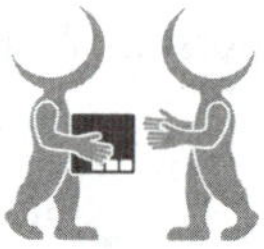

- Stand up immediately and face each other when one announces a gift.
- Don't reach out before the announcer takes out the gift.
- Receive the gift with both hands, smile and make eye contact. Then hold the gift with your left hand (large gift could be put down), and shake hands with right hand to thank the gift-giver.
- If a gift list (or a painting/a calligraphy) is provided, read it carefully from the beginning to the end immediately.

1.2 Etiquette in giving gifts

Gift-giving is a common social etiquette in business world. The skills of gift-giving should be focused on gaining communication effects.

- Both parties should try to give gifts of equal value. The similar item of the same category is a proper choice. For example, when one gives you a piece of painting works, you could reciprocate with calligraphy works.
- Consider gift-recipient's preferences and needs. A good gift is to one's liking, such as a latest best-seller for a book lover, or a stylish cosmetic product, or an accessory for a lady who loves fashion.
- The gifts should be packaged exquisitely. A beautiful gift packaging can add value of the gift, and show respect and sincerity. **NO** white or black is used in package for a Chinese.
- Remove the price tag and attach a note or business card.

1.3 Etiquette in refusing gifts

Generally speaking, refusing a gift is not appropriate. However, it happens sometimes, and some skills could be used to avoid embarrassing situations.

- When returning the gift, make sure that the gift should **NEVER BE OPENED** and be returned **WITHIN 24 HOURS**.
- How to say **NO** politely in English? Here are some expressions to refuse politely.

Saying NO to the gift

— It is really against policy. But I do appreciate your thinking of me/us.

— How nice! But I've already had one.

— Thank you/Thanks for your kindness! But I really can't accept it.

谢谢！但是这有违我们的公司规定。

谢谢！但是我真的不能接受。

Saying NO without specific reasons

— I wish I could make it work.

— Unfortunately, it's not a good time.

— I wish there were two of me, but I can't.

— Maybe another time.

不好意思！我不能接受。

2. Different Customs of Gifting Between China and Other Countries

2.1 Thank-you notes

Giving a thank-you note is considered to be polite after receiving gifts in English-speaking countries, while the Chinese prefer verbal thanks instead of a written form of gratitude.

2.2 Unpacking gifts in person

It is a tradition in English-speaking countries to unpack a gift in person, praise it, and show gratitude by giving a hug to the gift-giver. In the contrast, Chinese people usually do not open a gift on the spot.

2.3 Numbers

When giving gifts, the quantity of some numbers should be considered cautiously. Generally speaking, the Westerners prefer numbers FOUR and SEVEN while Chinese favor numbers SIX, EIGHT, NINE, and TEN.

Some nations in the west worship number four, believing that the four is a symbol of the power of fairness and justice. But in Chinese it is particularly a taboo about number FOUR because of its homonym with the unlucky word of death.

2.4 Colors

Knowledge of colors in different cultural backgrounds will be helpful in alternating an appropriate gift in business.

Red is a traditional color for festivities in China, representing joy and good luck. While in English, red is associated with blood, violence or loss, such as red ruin (火灾), red light (危险信号), red cent (一文不值), be in the red (负债、赤字).

White in China is the color of mourning and grief in funeral rites. The family members and friends of the deceased wear white clothes to express their condolences. However, in English-speaking countries, white is the color of wedding dress, representing the oath of innocence and flawlessness.

3. Gifts in Business with China's Unique Cultural Traditions

3.1 Tea

Tea, the most popular beverage since ancient China, is one of China's traditional specialties. Traditional tea from China falls into five major categories, i.e., green tea, black tea, Oolong tea, brick tea and jasmine tea. Modern Chinese nowadays also favor ginseng tea, scented tea, fruit tea, Babao tea, etc. Any kind could be a good gift to foreign business partners.

以下是有代表性的茶品种，可为赠礼佳品：

绿茶类：河南信阳毛尖、杭州西湖龙井、江苏吴县洞庭山碧螺春、安徽黄山毛峰。

红茶类：四川的川红、安徽的祁门红茶、云南的滇红。

乌龙茶类：福建安溪铁观音、台湾冻顶乌龙、福建武夷山大红袍。

茉莉花茶类：广西横州茉莉花茶、福建福州龙团珠茉莉花茶。

3.2 Silk products

China is the first producer of silk in the world and silk production was started about 4,500 years ago. Silk products from China are so popular that a trip to China could not be a complete one without a gift of silk products.

以下丝绸产品为常见的赠礼佳品：

丝巾、丝绸画、真丝领带、真丝衬衫

3.3 Chinese crafts

Chinese crafts are very popular in the world, such as wood and stone carving (木雕，石雕), antique porcelain (古代瓷器), brocade (织锦), and Tang tri-color glazed ceramics (唐三彩).

3.4 Crafts of Peking Opera

Popular both home and abroad, Peking Opera is a performing art with a unique form of its own, combining traditional Chinese music, poetry, singing, recitation, dancing, acrobatics and martial arts. For many foreigners, the singing, costumes and facial makeup are beautiful, mysterious and charming. A variety of crafts of Peking Opera could be a perfect gift to them.

3.5 Local specialties

People love delicious food, and it will never go wrong to give food as a gift. Universally recognized as one of the great cuisines in the world, Chinese food in all its variety and complexity is unquestionably one of the finest pleasure to experience. With the development of food preservation technology, local specialties could be gifted to business partners and be brought back to their hometown to share with families and friends.

4. Gifting Etiquette in Other Countries

USA

Office supplies can be used as suitable gifts. And specialties with Chinese features are very popular for American people.

European countries

French people like champagne, brandy, candy, perfume, books and art works. British people like flowers, wine, handicrafts and chocolates.

Arab countries

Pay attention to Arab religion. Don't give wine to them and never give gifts to a woman directly but through her father or husband.

Exercise 章节练习

1. Discussion

In April, 2023, French president Macron visited China. China has given France two national gifts: Luoyang peony and Chinese Go and Chess board made of bamboo and camphor wood (香樟木). Why did our Chinese government choose these two gifts? Discuss it with your teammates and try to figure out the profound implication.

2. Role play

Step 1: Design a business card. You can make up all the information on the card except your name.

Step 2: Work in pairs to discuss how to improve the two business cards.

Step 3: Work with two partners. Two will play the roles of two business persons who meet for the first time. The third one plays the role of the assistant who is to introduce the two business persons to each other. Group members can take turns to play different roles.

Step 4: Perform the role play in front of the other fellow students.

Step 5: When seeing a performance, finish the following assessment chart by scoring each point. (10 points for each)

Step 6: When each group finishes their performance, the audiences should offer their comments.

Performance	Group 1	Group 2	Group 3
1. a proper greeting way			
2. the assistant's correct introducing order			
3. the appropriate conversation between the two business persons			
4. the proper etiquette in exchanging business cards			
5. the proper etiquette in receiving business cards			
6. the appropriate language used			

Chapter Two Etiquette in Walking and Cars 行进礼仪与乘车礼仪

学习任务

1. 了解商务场合中行进时不同的礼仪。
2. 了解商务乘车时应遵循的礼仪。

I. Etiquette in Walking 行进礼仪

Contents:

1. Daily walking
2. Walking up or down stairs
3. Walking in or out of an elevator
4. Walking in or out of a room

Warm-up:

1. Have you ever noticed people's daily walking? Could you describe some walking details of different people and different occasions?

2. On business occasions, some etiquette in walking should be paid attention to. Could you use some examples to illustrate what you have known about the etiquette in walking?

1. Daily Walking

个人的日常行走仪态准则，已在本书前文“仪态”章节中进行介绍。本章节将具体介绍不同情景中行进的其他规范。

两人或多人行进时，同辈同级别的人，无须过多关注行进时的位序；但与尊长、上级或宾客行进时，特别是在较为正式的场合，要遵照以下原则：

(1) When two people walk in a parallel line, always let the senior people, superiors, ladies and guests be on the right side or the inner side; when two people walk one in front of the other, always let the senior people, superiors, ladies and guests walk in front; when three or more people walk together, the most honorable people always walk in the middle and the front, the second honorable people walk in the right side and the third honorable people walk in the left, with other people walk behind.

两人行走，并行时，以右或内侧为尊，以左或外侧为卑，前后行进时，以前方为尊；三人或多人并行，以中为尊，右边次之，左边更次之；多人行走，以前为尊，以后为卑。

图 1　男士走在女士右侧，为地位高者

图 2　男士右边女士地位高于男士左边女士

(2) On business occasions, the guide always walks in the left front of the guests while the attendant walks in the left behind the guests.

在商务场合中，陪同者和引领者在行进时所走位置也有相应的准则。

引领者走在宾客的左前方，陪同者则位于宾客的左侧稍偏后的位置。

引领客人观看橱窗或展品时，应让宾客更靠近橱窗或展品，引领讲解者则位于宾客前方稍靠外的位置进行讲解。

2. Walking up or down Stairs

单人或与人同行时，均应纵列行走，不应多人并排；不应推挤他人。

当引领他人上下楼梯时，男女引领者须遵循不同引领原则。

(1) When a male guide is guiding a male guest in a business occasion, the basic norm is: The guide walks behind the guest when going up stairs but in front of the guest when going down stairs.

引领他人上下楼梯，尤其是正式社交中，男性引领者陪同男性尊长、上级、宾客时，上楼梯时应走在其侧后方，可做出引领手势；下楼梯时应走在其侧前方陪同引领。

If the guest is a woman, the male guide always walks in front when going up or down stairs.

当引领者为男性，宾客为男女都有时，要根据最重要宾客（一般走在最前面）的性别，来决定引领者走在前面还是后面。

(2) If the guide is a woman, she should always walk behind the guest when going up or down stairs.

3. Walking in or out of an Elevator

When walking in or out of an elevator, you should enter the elevator according to the waiting order and step out one by one. But when walking with the senior people, superiors, ladies and guests in or out of an elevator, you should follow the two principles below:

（1）后进后出：

电梯内有管理者时，陪同尊长、上级或客人进出电梯，应主动后进后出。

电梯内无管理者时，陪同者应先进入电梯，按住开门键等待客人进入；出电梯时，应按住开门键，等待客人全部走出电梯后，再走出电梯。

（2）先进后出：

4. Walking in or out of a Room

When walking in or out of a room in public places, business occasions or work places, you should pay attention to several norms.

(1) When guiding the senior people, superiors, ladies or other distinguished guests into or out of a room, use your hand (not foot, elbow, knees or other body parts) to open or close the door gently for them; always let them enter or leave the room first.

陪同尊长、上级或者客人进出房间时，都应以手控制门呈开启状态（若门的开启方向同行进方向一致，则先行一步开门等待），待客人等先进出房间。

(2) When entering or leaving a room with other people, especially when senior people, superiors, ladies or other distinguished guests are in the room, you should always face the people in the room.

房间有人的情况下，进门时要始终面朝对方，进入后关门时也应尽量面朝房间里的人；出门时，在到达房门开门前，应尽量面朝房间里的人，不要以背示人；转身出门后关门时，仍要面对房间里的人关上房门。

(3) Generally, you should let senior people, superiors, ladies and guests enter and leave the room first and hold the door for them.

如果出入房间时正巧有人与自己往相反方向出入房间，应侧身礼让，先出后进。但若对方是长者、上级、女士或者客人，则让他们先行。

II. Etiquette in Cars 乘车礼仪

Contents:

1. Arrangement of cars
2. Different arrangements of car seats
3. Orders of getting on or off a car

Warm-up:

How to arrange the car seats in a business trip?

Mia is a secretary of the general manager of a company. She is taking guests by car to a restaurant for a reception banquet. The guests are a couple—Mr. Smith and his wife Mrs. Smith. Which seat should Mr. Smith take? Please mark the seat in the following picture.

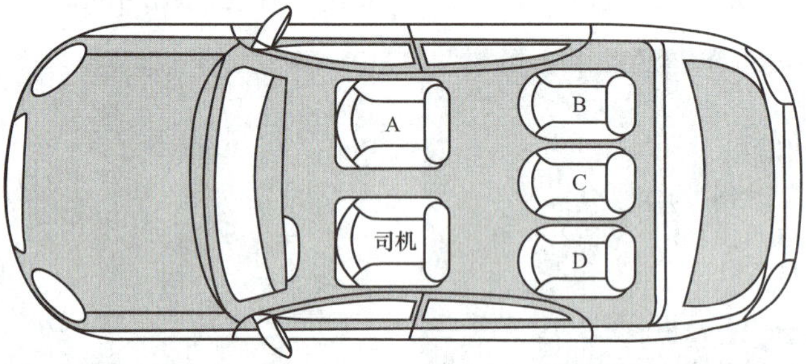

What if in a seven-seater car, which seat should Mr. Smith take? Please mark the seat in the following picture.

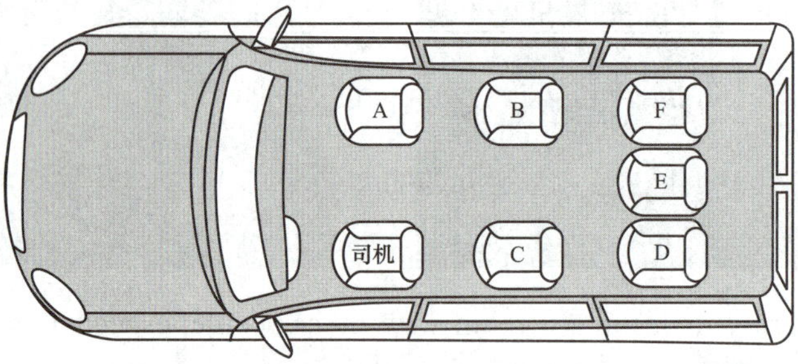

1. Arrangement of Cars

The number of cars should be determined according to the number of people on both sides.

The rules for arranging cars are as follows: The people in the car don't feel crowded while riding. A retinue of our side should be arranged in each car in order to greet and guide the way.

The general practice is that the riding order should be arranged according to the age or positions. The most senior foreign guests and the most senior leaders of our side will be sent in the first car, accompanied by a retinue (a secretary or an interpreter). Other foreign guests and other host personnel take the following cars.

2. Different Arrangements of Car Seats

When determining the rank of the car seats, you should take the following four factors into consideration: the driver, the type of the car, safety and the guests' own will.

2.1 The driver

2.1.1 When the owner, businessman himself, drives the car, the following examples will help to understand the seating rules:

主人亲自驾驶时，商务礼仪规定：前排为尊，右为尊。

a. A two-row five-seater car driven by the owner himself

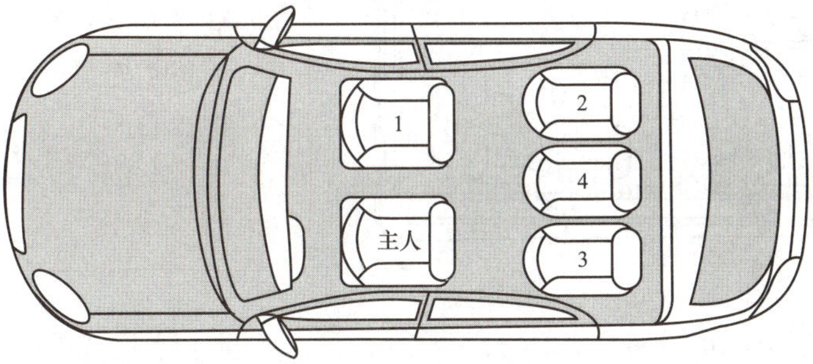

排座顺序：
1 副驾驶座
2 后排右座
3 后排左座
4 后排中座

b. A three-row seven-seater car driven by the owner himself

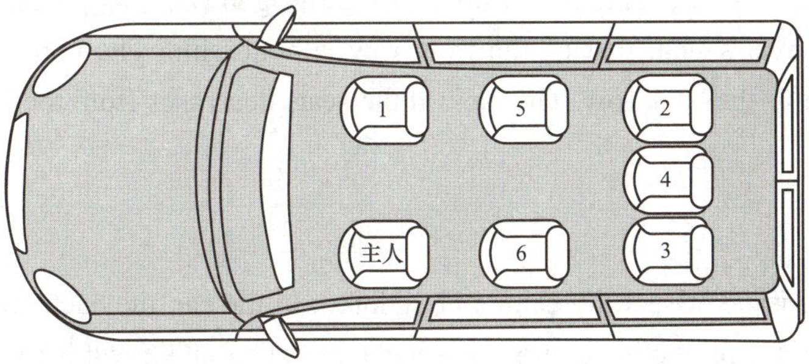

排座顺序：
1 副驾驶座
2 后排右座
3 后排左座
4 后排中座
5 中排右座
6 中排左座

2.1.2 When a full-time driver (专职司机) drives the car, the following examples will help to understand the seating rules:

> 专职司机亲自驾驶时，商务礼仪规定：后排为尊，右为尊。

a. A two-row five-seater car driven by the full-time driver

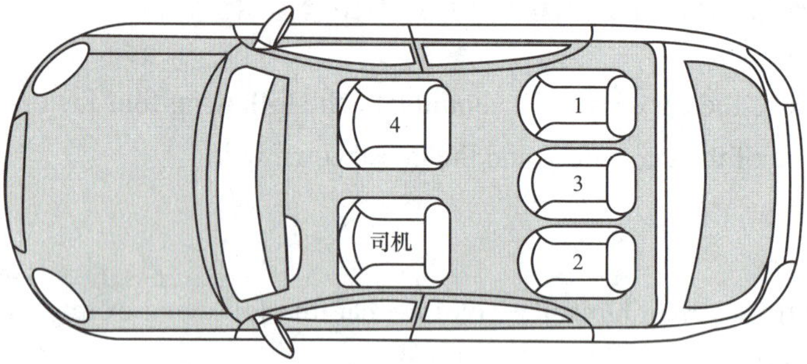

排座顺序：
1 后排右座
2 后排左座
3 后排中座
4 副驾驶座

b. A three-row seven-seater car driven by the full-time driver

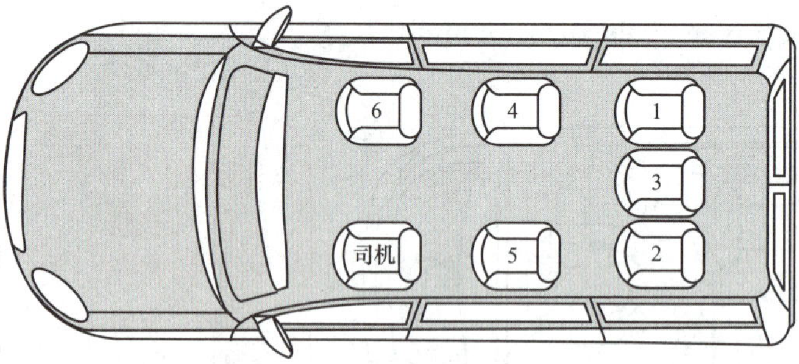

排座顺序：
1 后排右座
2 后排左座
3 后排中座
4 中排右座
5 中排左座
6 副驾驶座

2.2 Type of cars

The above rules are mainly applicable to two-row and three-row cars, but not applicable to other special types of cars.

When you receive group guests on business occasions, station wagon (旅行车) is usually used. The first row after the driver's seat, that is, the front row is honorable. The honorable degree decreases from the front to the back row. The rank of the seats decreases from the right side of each row to the left.

2.3 Safety

When you take the car, the issue of security cannot be ignored. In the car, the back seat is safer than the front seat. The least safe seat is the front passenger seat. The safest seat is the left seat in the back. According to international practice, a woman should not normally be allowed to sit in the front passenger seat when riding a car driven by a full-time driver.

2.4 The guests' own will

For the rank of the car seat, you shouldn't be so predictable. On formal occasions, you should guide guests to the honorable seat. But it doesn't matter which seat the guests take if they have their preference. Wherever the guest sits, the seat will be seen as an honorable seat.

3. Orders of Getting on or off a Car

By convention, the retinue should take the initiative to open the door and invite foreign guests to get on the car first. And then the retinue walks around the back of the car to the other side to avoid crossing in front of the guest seat. Finally, the retinue takes the passenger seat.

When getting off the car, the retinue should get off first and open the door for the foreign guests. If there is someone waiting to open the door, the retinue can get off at the same time as the foreign guests.

Exercise 章节练习

1. Role play

Step 1: Divide the students into several groups to practice the etiquette in walking they have learned in this chapter. Make sure each group has 2-4 students and involves boys and girls. The students themselves decide which role they want to play, the guest, the guiding person or the accompanying person.

Step 2: Let each group practice all the walking etiquette and pay attention to the details. For example, when walking up or down stairs, should the guiding person walk in front or behind the guest?

Step 3: Randomly choose 2 or 3 groups to do the presentation. When the group are on stage, the other students choose which scene to simulate and watch carefully to find the mistakes the group may have.

Step 4: The teacher comments on the performance.

2. Practice

Practice in groups to simulate sitting and getting on and off the car. The following are several situations, which can be practiced and arranged by students respectively.

1) Three for the foreign side (marketing manager, assistant marketing manager, secretary), two for Chinese side (interpreter, driver), they take one car driven by the owner.

2) Five for the foreign side (deputy general manager, marketing manager, assistant marketing manager, secretary A, secretary B), two for Chinese side (interpreter, driver), they take one car driven by the full-time driver.

Chapter Three

Etiquette in Conversation

谈话礼仪

学习任务

1. 了解交谈的要求和特点。
2. 了解有效交谈的原则和禁忌。
3. 认识交谈中非语言因素的影响。
4. 掌握正确的称呼方式。
5. 了解如何选择谈话话题和交谈技巧。

一人之辩重于九鼎之宝，三寸之舌强于百万之师

——《战国策·东周》

Speaking is a crucial means of expressing concepts and emotions, which is also the key tool of establishing personal relationships. Please do remember that courtesy demands reciprocity. Talking should be considered as an art form; attitude and tone do matter. The importance of conversation will be discussed in this chapter.

有人谈起话来滔滔不绝，容不得其他人插嘴，把别人都当成了自己的学生；有人为显示自己的伶牙俐齿，总是喜欢用夸张的语气来谈话，甚至不惜危言耸听；有人以自己为中心，完全不顾他人的喜怒哀乐，一天到晚谈的只有自己。这些人给人的只是傲慢、放肆、自私的印象，因为不懂得尊重别人。

In human history, communication, like labor, life, has been entitled as one of those social phenomena.

I. Requirements and Characteristics of Conversation 交谈的要求与特点

1. Requirements of Conversation

1.1 Humble attitude

诚恳、亲切的态度是谈话成功的重要因素。在商务交往中，言未出而态度先行，良好的态度将降低谈话者的戒心，减少成见，可以起到事半功倍的效果。

1.2 Appropriate voice, speed and tone

中国有句成语叫作“理直气壮”，其实在大多数交际场合即便“理直”也无须“气壮”。

Keep your voice down, and keep it slow.

1.3 Clear and understandable expression

谈话的基本功能是进行信息的交流，所以你至少要让对方知道你在说什么。

Speak your customer’s mother tongue, or the language that both of you can understand.

In China, we prefer Putonghua!

1.4 Proper manners

谈话并不是单一的说话，“谈”涉及的不仅是双方话语上的交流，还有理念的传达。恰如其分的肢体语言（body language）能起到辅助的作用。反之，过多的、夸张的手势只会凸显说话人的紧张与不安。

2. Characteristics of Conversation

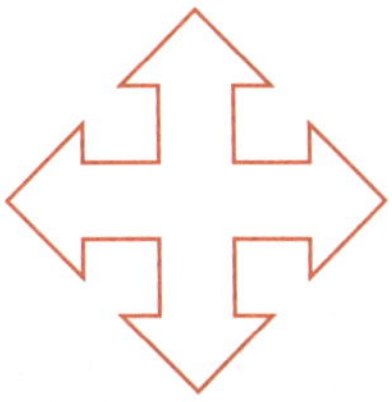

Most significantly, be real, and be natural.

II. Principles, Factors and Taboos in Conversation 交谈的原则、因素与禁忌

1. Principles

1.1 Addressing others appropriately

A proper and appropriate salutation will not only make the other side feel comfortable, but also easily narrow the distance between the two sides of the conversation and become the cornerstone of further exchanges.

1.2 Acknowledging others promptly

When the opinions of both sides are similar or basically consistent, one side should confirm the views timely and pertinently, and the other side should also express his approval. This kind of two-way exchange is easy to promote the relationship of both sides so as to lay a good foundation for reaching an agreement.

1.3 Showing amiable attitude and using decent language

Make conversations naturally and confidently. Be amiable in attitude and decent in language. Do not use too many gestures or movements. The content of your conversation generally does not involve unpleasant things.

1.4 Paying attention to speed, tone, and volume

Try to present your ideas at a steady and moderate pace during the conversation. On certain occasions, you can change the speed of speech to attract the other side's attention and enhance the effect of expression. Daily conversations should be stated in a normal tone, maintaining a moderate volume that can be clearly heard by the other side without causing resentment.

2. "5W" Principles

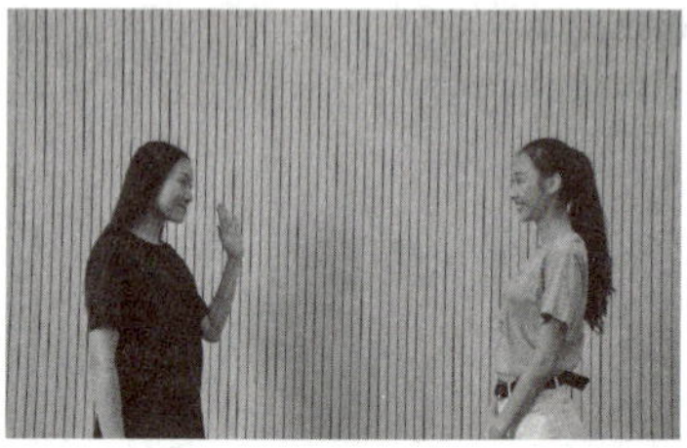

——Who同谁交谈

——Why为什么要交谈

——Which采取哪一种方式进行交谈

——Where是在哪里进行交谈

——What期望得到什么样的交谈效果

3. Six Factors (SOFTEN)

- 微笑（SMILE）
- 开放的姿态（OPEN POSTURE）
- 身体前倾（FORWARD LEANING）
- 音调（TONE）
- 目光交流（EYE COMMUNICATION）
- 点头（NODDING）

4. Ten Taboos

Stop

Being inactive	Glib tongue
Interrupting	Garrulity
Inappropriate topics	Sophistry
Being bitter and sarcastic	Dirty talk
Talebearing	Frivolity

III. Non-Verbal Language in Conversation 交谈中的非言语语言

1. Gesture: 优雅的坐姿站姿，搭配适当而不浮夸的手部动作

2. Facial Expression: 切不可东张西望，面部表情不宜过多

3. Eye Contact: 三角策略

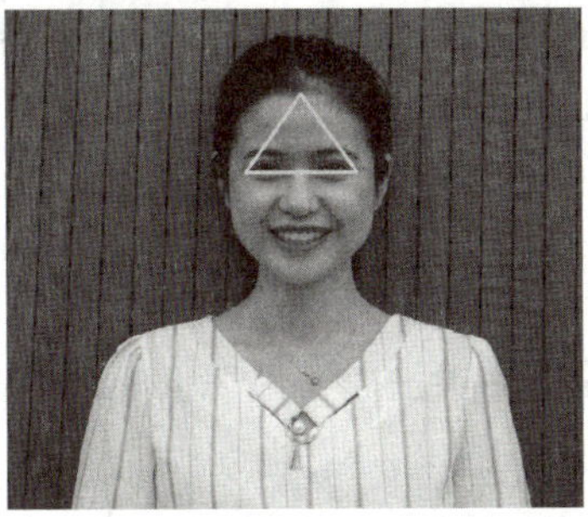

Professional Eye Contact/Power Gaze: negotiation/ conference

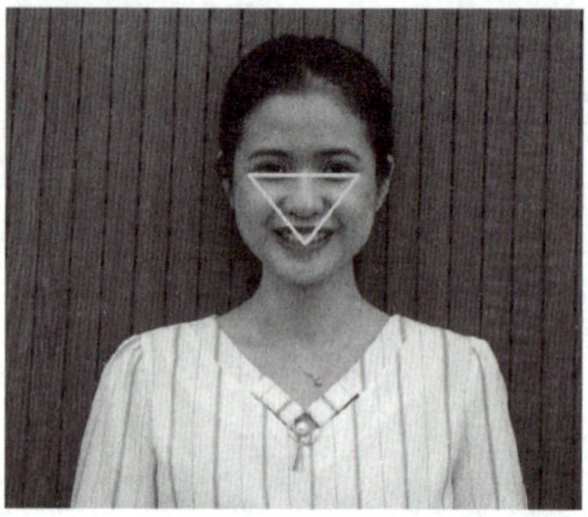

V touch/Social Gaze: friends/colleagues

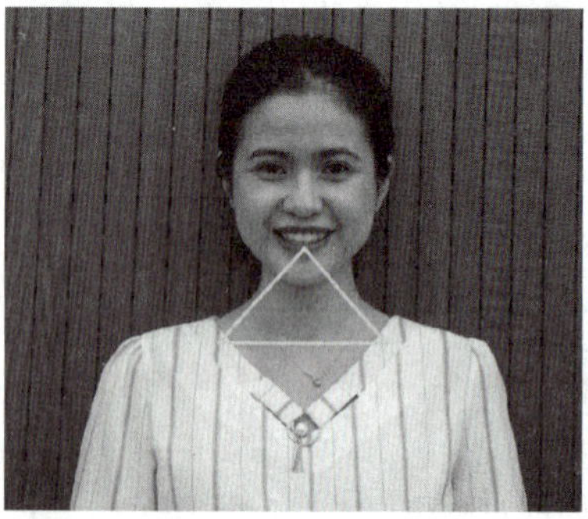

Intimate Gaze: relatives/lovers

4. Distance: 根据场景、对象选择适宜的交谈距离

➔ **美国人类学家爱德华·霍尔（Edward Hall）博士提出人际交往的四种距离：**

—Intimate distance: <0.5 m	父母、夫妻、情侣
—Personal distance: 0.5 m–1.5 m	联系密切的熟人、朋友
—Social distance: 1.5 m–3 m	商务、公务场合
—Public distance: >3 m	公开演讲时

IV. Salutation 称呼

1. Principles

Appellation is the door to business contact. Right appellation will do more with less. And proper appellation must abide by the principle of appellation etiquette. The basic principle of appellation etiquette is courtesy and propriety.

1.1 Courtesy

Everyone wants to be respected by others. Proper appellation is a way of expressing respect for others and showing that you are polite and cultured.

In business communication, respectful appellation should be used when addressing each other. 常见的尊称有："您""贵""大""高""尊"。

1.2 Propriety

In business communication, it is necessary to choose the appropriate appellation in view of the object, the occasion, the relationship between the two sides, etc. When greeting a large number of people, closeness and title should be paid attention to. 一般以先亲后疏、先长后幼、先高后低为宜。

2. Techniques

2.1 Remembering others' names

2.2 Addressing others according to different business circumstances

2.3 Being cautious when you first meet someone

2.4 Being careful even if you are familiar

在商务场合，准确地记住和称呼他人的名字，会使对方倍感亲切、自然，有助于缩短双方的心理距离。商务称呼应该随着不同的商务环境而变化。在中国，常用的称呼有先生/女士、师傅、老师等。在西方，一般对男子称先生，对女子称夫人、女士、小姐等。初次与某人见面时，要谨慎地称呼对方。在中国，如果对方有一定的职务，要称呼"姓+职务"。在西方，最常用的是"Mr. + 姓氏""Mrs. + 姓氏""Ms.+姓氏""Miss + 姓氏"。随着往来次数的增加，彼此之间变得非常熟悉。切记，不要以为是熟人就可以随便，这样会影响双方的沟通效果。

3. Appellation in Formal Occasions

在正式场合，我们一般会使用职务(position)、职称(professional titles)、泛尊(common respectful appellation)、职业（career）或姓名（name）来称呼别人，以表示尊重。然而，有些时候简单的称呼会无意中冒犯别人，带来一些麻烦。

4. Taboos

4.1 替代性（demonstrative pronoun/salutation）

因不了解对方，称呼对方的方式过于随意，或者拿对方的特征（比如身体上的）来作为称呼。

例如：喂！
　　那个扎马尾辫的！
　　嗨！
　　那边那个……

4.2 地域性（regional salutation）

有些称呼是带有地域色彩的，在当地作为泛指的称呼，没有具体的实际意义。

例如：伙计、爱人
　　美女、帅哥
　　大妹子、兄弟

4.3 蔑视性（disparaging salutation）

某些称呼明显带有歧视或者蔑视，已经构成对对方的伤害甚至侮辱的，特别注意绝对要避免。

例如：The old man→老头　　the bald→秃头
　　黑鬼（Negro）　　洋人（the foreigners）

V. Topics and Strategies 交谈的话题和策略

1. Topics

1.1 Principles of good topics

亚里士多德曾经指出：交谈由谈话者、听话者、主题等三个要素组成，“要达到施加影响的目的，就必须关注此三要素”。

话题应注意：

Designated
Elegant
Comfortable
Adept

1.2 Topics that should NOT be mentioned

1.2.1 Politics issues

Whether in China or other countries, avoiding political topics is strongly recommended, because normally speaking, people who are involved in the conversation consider these topics as “sensitive”.

1.2.2 Religion issues

Sometimes, it is hard for the business partners to know the religious background of one another. Misunderstandings may occur if religion is brought out.

1.2.3 Privacy issues

Issues like marriage status, age, weight, personal income, family problems are not welcomed in the conversations between business partners. Those topics mentioned above may lead to personal antipathy.

2. Strategies

2.1 Being sincere, amiable and decent

Which one is better?

A：就这么决定！你说什么也不能动摇我的想法！

B：你所说的固然也有道理，但我真的已经决定了。

卖关子？
插科打诨？

2.2 A good listener, a good speaker

- ✧ Use your sense of humor.
- ✧ Use your emotion.
- ✧ Use proper compliments.
- ✧ Learn and dare to say NO.

幽默既不是毫无意义的插科打诨，也不是没有分寸的卖关子，耍嘴皮。幽默要在入情入理之中，引人发笑，给人启迪，需要一定的素质和修养。

VI. Two Most Important Types of Face-to-Face Conversation 面对面交谈的两种重要类型

Face-to-face communication plays a remarkable role in social intercourse, and it cannot be replaced by any other means of communication. Moreover, daily greeting and small talk are the most common types.

“听其言，观其行”

1. Daily Greeting

1.1 Some basic requirements

礼仪是我们生活中不可或缺的一环，日常交往中的打招呼有时候会给别人留下积极或消极的印象，甚至影响别人对你的印象。那么，我们在打招呼时有哪些基本事项需要注意呢？

1.1.1 Greeting others on your own initiative

打招呼是联络感情的手段，是沟通心灵的方式和增进友谊的纽带。要有效地打招呼，首先应该积极主动地跟别人打招呼。

1.1.2 Who should take the initiative to say hello?

男性先向女性致意，年轻的不管男女均应首先向年长者致意，下级应向上级致意。两对夫妇见面，女性先互相致意，然后男性分别向对方的妻子致意，最后男性互相致意。

1.1.3 When you meet someone on the street

在大街上打招呼，三四步远是最好的距离，男子可欠身或点头，如果戴着帽子须摘去。与人打招呼时，忌叼着烟卷或把手插在衣袋里。

1.1.4　Are there any rules of greeting for women?

女性在各种生活场景中，均应主动微笑点头致意，以示亲和。

对熟人不打招呼，或不应答向你打招呼的人都是失礼的行为。

1.1.5　If you encounter the following circumstances, there is some advice for you.

- 与西方人打招呼时避免中式用语“你上哪儿去”“你干什么去”等，在西方人看来，有涉人私事之嫌，是失礼的语言；更不应说“吃饭了吗”，否则被误认为你想邀请他一起吃饭。
- 与少数民族及信奉宗教的人打招呼应根据当地的宗教信仰及招呼习惯。

1.2　Common expressions of greeting in Chinese and English

“你吃了吗？”
“你干什么去？”

How are you?
How’s it going?

“你在哪儿发财？”
“你这段时间忙吗？”
“你好!”

What’s up? Wha’s happening?
How’s everything?
What’s new?
Good to see you!

2. Small Talks

2.1 Variety

寒暄，有人认为就是随便聊两句，有人说它其实有着很重要的作用。其实，寒暄是一种问候，更是一种应酬的方式，恰如其分的寒暄并不容易掌握。

2.1.1 Running into acquaintance on the road

If you come across acquaintances in public places, you should greet them. Sometimes, you may say hello and leave, but you may also stop and talk for a few minutes.

如有急事要办，来不及多说时，应和对方说清楚再离开，这是人际交往的基本礼貌。

2.1.2 Before the conference

This kind of small talk paves the way for formal conference. You can start with “Hello” “Please come in” “Please sit down”, etc.

2.1.3 Small talk on the phone

Rules on the phone are similar to the ones mentioned above.

如是见过面但不太熟的商务伙伴，寒暄时可谈一些近况或上次见面的愉快情景。没见过面，寒暄一般会以问候和赞美或者聊双方都熟识的人、事为主。

2.2 What kind of topics can be chosen when you conduct a small talk?

The basis of small talk is your content. Basically speaking, topics boths parties are interested in are welcomed, so that they can discuss and exchange ideas.

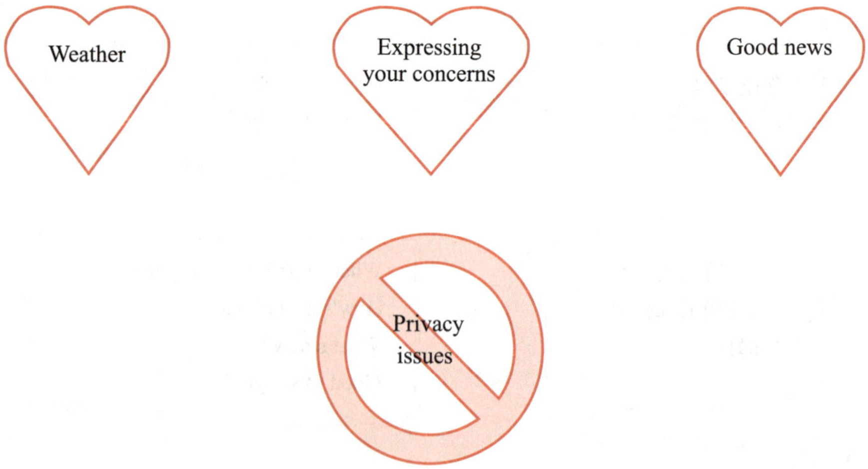

Exercise 章节练习

1. Question and discussion

What should we pay attention to if we meet an acquaintance, or a business partner?

2. Scan the QR codes to watch two video clips, and discuss the differences and importance of conducting conversations with different people.

Chapter Four

Communication Etiquette
通信礼仪

学习任务

1. 了解打电话的礼仪要求。
2. 了解书信往来的礼仪要求。
3. 了解发短信的礼仪要求。
4. 了解其他通信形式的礼仪要求。

Life-related issues involve etiquette in many ways. Communication is one of the main subjects of publicity, and also a kind of business. People communicate with each other via telephones, messages, emails, then their intentions, personalities, emotions and moods are conveyed. Both sides of the communication reveal their temperaments and cultural backgrounds, which is the communicative image.

通信：

（1）用书信互通消息，反映情况等；

（2）利用电波、光波等信号传送文字、图像等。

这里的“通信”，泛指利用纸质或电波、光波、电子等介质互通、传递信息的活动。

Communication etiquette refers to the regulations, requirements and customs that people have to follow in the communication. Due to the different communicative media with diverse purposes, there are four types of communication etiquette that will be introduced in this chapter.

I. Telephone Etiquette 电话礼仪

Contents:

1. The features of phone calls
2. Making and answering phone calls

生活中，您可曾遇到过这些情况：

*夜深人静，突然被一阵电话铃声惊醒……

*好不容易盼来了休假，却被一个个工作电话搅得兴致全无……

*世界杯期间，办公室一同事拿起电话就打："昨晚看球了吗……"

*单位正在召开一个重要会议，电话铃声却此起彼伏……

*过年过节各种祝福手机短信令人应接不暇，却不知谁人发送……

*手机由于某种原因丢了，最惨的是里面的数百条通讯录都没备份……

1. Features

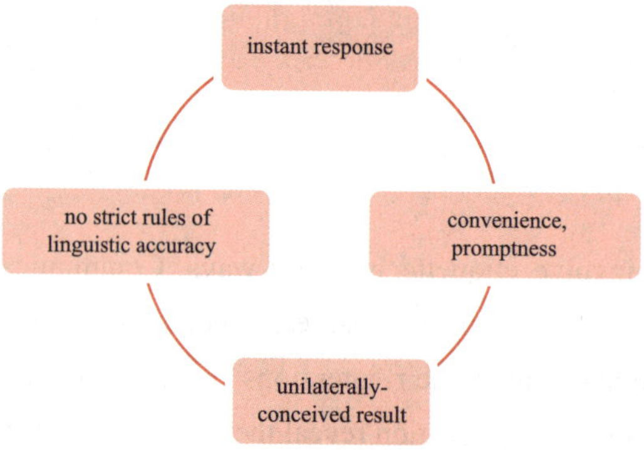

2. Two Categories: Making Calls and Answering Calls

2.1 Making a phone call

现如今，打电话是人们常用的一种沟通交流方式。电话使人们的联系更为方便、快捷。然而，你懂得如何打电话吗？

Tips：
求职办事不要在周一上午一上班或周五下午快下班时打。另外每天上班的前 2 个小时是电话高峰期，注意尽量避开。

2.1.1 Rules of Time

- After 8 a.m. — before 10 p.m.
- Business calls ONLY during business hours and weekdays
- Urgent calls among weekends: after 10 a.m.

2.1.2 Rules of duration: 3-Minute Principle

有话直说
废话少说
长话短说
无话不说

2.1.3 Content

1 • 问候

2 • 自报家门

3 • 具体事件

4 • 结束语

2.1.4 Attitude: being delightful

打电话时我们要保持喜悦的心情，这样会给对方留下极佳的印象。面部表情会影响声音的变化，即使在电话中，也要抱着“对方看着我”的心态去应对，让对方能够“听到”你的笑容。

2.2 Answering phone calls

人们常常会忽略接电话的礼仪，一声“喂，你好！”可以给对方留下良好的印象。除此之外，还有什么接电话礼仪需要注意呢？

2.2.1 Three-time principle: letting the phone ring for no more than three times

接听时间过早或过晚会让对方感到很仓促不受尊重，留下不好的印象。

2.2.2 Answering calls for someone else:

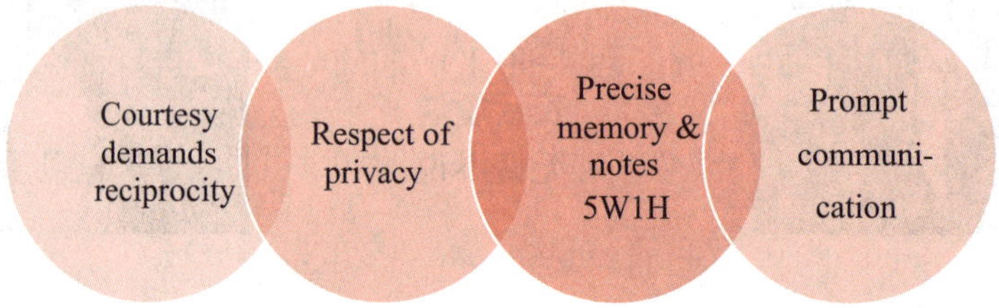

2.3 Other dos and don'ts

电话礼仪的掌握在商务场合是一把双刃剑。让我们一起来看看其他的注意事项吧！

2.3.1 Environment of making calls:

- Do choose a quiet and convenient environment with good signal.
- Do not make a phone call in a bus, supermarket, traditional market, or other noisy environments.

如果是座机，请轻放电话，否则那声响绝对把你前面给对方留下的好印象都抹掉。一定请对方先挂电话，应聘者不要着急挂电话。

2.3.2 Who should firstly hang up calls?

The seniors, the superiors, guests, ladies hang up first.

Or the caller hangs up first.

2.3.3 During your calls:

- No smoking, eating or drinking.
- Your laziness can be "heard". If you are lying on the couch and showing listless, your listener may know.
- Enthusiastic and gentle voice is preferable.
- Always be ready to take notes when you are on the phone.

常见错误用语	规范通话用语
喂！(YO!)	您好！(Hello!)
你是谁呀？(Who are you?)	请问您是哪位？(Who is calling, please?)
等下！(Wait!)	请您稍等片刻。(Please wait a moment.)
你找我什么事？(What do you want?)	请问您有什么事情？(What can I do for you?)
还有事吗？(Anything else?)	请问您还有其他事吗？(Is there anything else I can help you?)
我知道了。(I know I know.)	好的，您的信息我都记录下来了。(OK, I have written down all the information.)
什么？我没听清。(What? I cannot hear you.)	对不起，我没有听清您的话，请您再讲一遍。(Sorry, I couldn't catch what you said. Could you please say it again?)
你电话多少？(What is your number?)	对不起，请问您的电话是多少？(Excuse me, what's your phone number?)
挂了吧。(That is!)	再见！(Goodbye!)

II. Etiquette in Correspondence 书信礼仪

Contents:

1. Format of letters
2. Sending and receiving letters
3. The envelope

1. Format

1.1 Format of Chinese letters

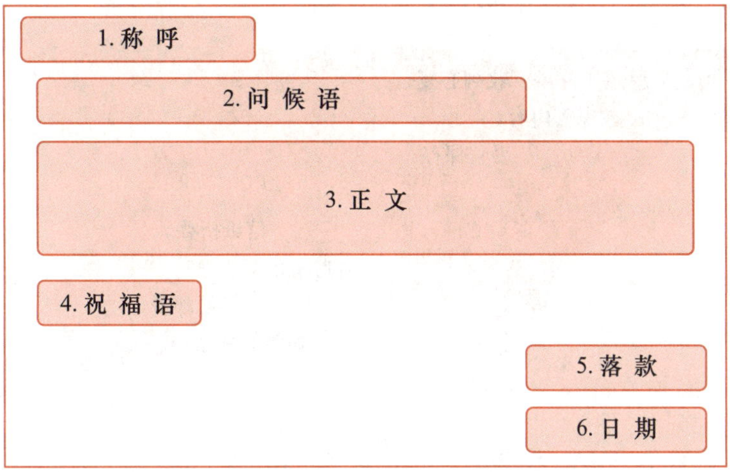

1.2 Format of English letters

1. Date 日期

2. Salutation 称谓
如:
*Dear Sir (or Madam),
*Dear Mr. (Ms./Mrs....),
*To whom it may concern,
*Dear ladies and gentlemen,

3. Body of letter 信件正文
(the first paragraph)（第一段）
(the second paragraph)（第二段）

4. Closing 结尾敬辞
如：*Yours sincerely, *Regrads,

5. Name (typed) 姓名（打字）

6. Signature (hand-writing) 亲笔签名

2. Sending and Receiving Letters

Remember:

收到必复；
保密内容；
妥善保存。

信纸折叠；
信封粘合；
付足邮费；
邮票的粘贴。

3. The Envelope

III. Etiquette in Sending Messages 短信礼仪

Contents:

1. Time to send messages
2. Content of the messages
3. Punctual reply

1. Time

Working hours: 9 a.m. to 5 p.m. (weekdays except Monday, for Monday is the meeting day in lots of companies)

Please do send the work-related messages during working hours, especially for foreigners; they are not willing to mix private life and professional life.

P.S. Do not forget your signature!

2. Content

Keep it simple, brief, and relevant.

Verbose expressions and "Holiday Words" are unnecessary. Please state your ideas and requirements directly in order to save time. Do not run in circles!

3. Reply in Time

People may feel disrespectful if they wait for the reply too long.

Promptness is important for both parties; sometimes business opportunities will be lost due to your delay.

IV. Etiquette in Using Instant Communicative Tools 社交软件礼仪

Contents:

1. Email
2. Other chatting tools

1. Email

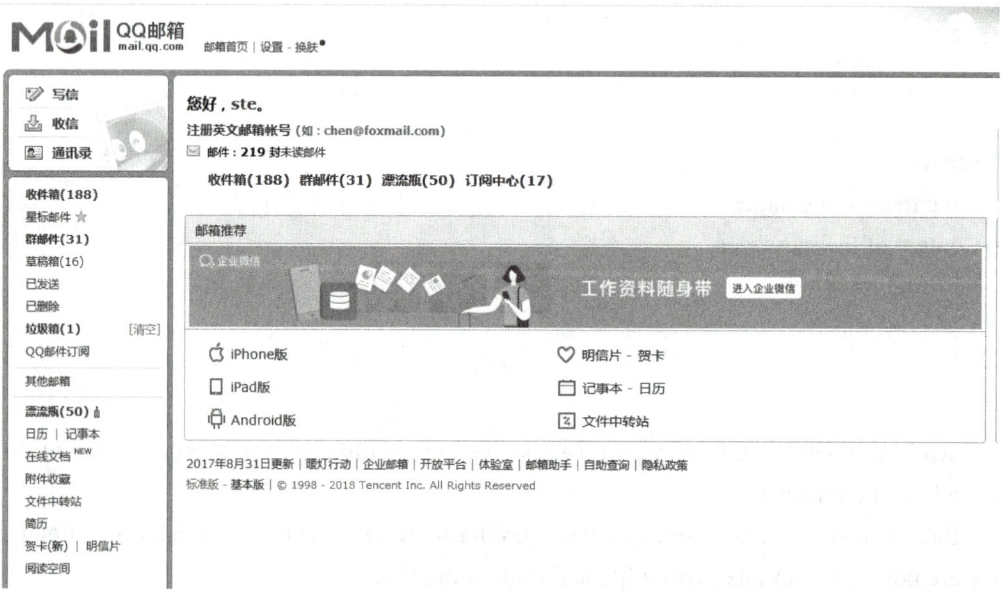

1.1 Format

To:	Charlesgreen@sohu.com
From:	Sallypeng@163.com
CC:	
Subject:	Letter of Application

Dear Mr. Green,

I am writing to apply for the post of HR manager assistant as I have learned it from the advertisement in *Global Times*.

I graduated from Guangxi University in 2018, majoring in secretary. I have strong interest in this field and want to begin my career in your company. I would be very grateful if you offer me a chance to have an interview.

I am looking forward to meeting you.

Yours sincerely,

Sally Peng

Enc. CV

1.2 Requirements

1.2.1 Normative email content

The subject line of the email must be written so that the other side can see the content of the email at a glance. The content should be as concise as possible, with space between paragraphs. A greeting and signature should be part of an email, which is a sign of respect for the recipient.

1.2.2 Moderate font size

The font size should be moderate. Do not choose a font that is difficult for the other person to read. If the email is written in English, be careful not to use all capital letters.

1.2.3 Proper use of attachments

If the content of the email is not long, send the email in the body form. Files with large amounts of pictures, videos or texts can be sent as attachments. If you want to send multiple files or large files, you can compress them before sending them.

1.2.4 Answering emails promptly

Open your inbox regularly to check new messages. You'd better reply on the day of receipt to ensure the timely transmission of information and the smooth development of work.

1.2.5 Organizing email regularly

You should organize your inbox regularly, save and delete different emails separately.

1.2.6 Respecting privacy

Avoid sending personal emails from your work email address. Some people don't want their email addresses to appear in other people's emails, so when sending a group email, respect for other people's privacy should be considered.

1.3 Other dos

1.3.1 Providing a title for your file in attachment

1.3.2 Remembering to use RAR file

太多条目的附件请用压缩包，文件较大的附件请分成几个小文件。

2. Other Chatting Tools in Business

第三方的在线或离线客户端很多，现在你有越来越多的方法来进行聊天了。有这么多的即时聊天工具选择，你可能会很难抉择到底用哪一个。从 MSN 到 QQ，再到 WeChat，还有在国外使用的 Meebo, WhatsAPP, Chaptous，即时聊天工具在人们的生活中越来越重要了。甚至在商务沟通的时候，越来越多的即时聊天工具被使用。但是，我们在使用时有没有忘记什么呢？

2.1 Choice of your content

- Talk about work-related issues.
- No privacy (financial situation, family, marriage status, etc.).
- For females, do not ask anything about their age, weight or marriage.

2.2 Choice of your language: civilized

- Simple, cordial but formal.
- Do not use cyber language.
- Try to use words, rather than voice message.

2.3 Using emojis if necessary

- Applying emojis, pictures, even cartoons appropriately may benefit the communication.
- Emojis should be carefully chosen based on mutual relationship as well as the context of conversations.

Exercise 章节练习

Role play

Directions: Please form a group of 2-4, and make a telephone call with your group members based on the etiquette learned in this chapter.

Chapter Five Dining Etiquette 餐桌礼仪

学习任务

1. 了解商务宴请的不同形式。
2. 了解在不同宴请形式中的礼仪要求。

Business dinners are important parts of international business interaction. They can be divided into different kinds in terms of occasions and levels, such as formal banquet, informal dinner, buffet, reception, cocktail party, tea party, working lunch and so on. The purposes of business dinners are varied: welcoming, discussing business matters, socializing and experiencing special food culture. In terms of meals in a day, there are breakfast, lunch and supper, among which the supper is the most formal. The purposes, guests, levels are essential to business dinners. In this chapter, business dinners such as formal dinner, working lunch, and buffet will be introduced.

I. Formal Banquet 宴会

Contents:

1. Seating and table etiquette in China
2. Seating and table etiquette in western countries

Warm-up:

Choose the best answer to each question.

1. Which side is the privileged seat in a formal Chinese meal nowadays?

A. Left. B. Right.

2. Which is the least favorable to most foreigners?

A. Sliced beef in hot chili oil. B. Braised pork balls in brown sauce.

C. Honey chicken wings. D. Poached goose intestine.

3. What is served last in a Western meal?

A. Dessert. B. Drink. C. Soup. D. Salad.

4. Who should be seated next to a gentleman in a Western meal?

A. His wife. B. His male friend.

C. His female friend. D. A female stranger.

Chinese culture:

Yuan and round table

Besides its literal meaning "round, circle", *Yuan*, in Chinese traditional culture, means being complete, comprehensive and harmonious. It is a significant image in the life of Chinese and also a key factor to understand Chinese culture. Chinese like round things, which can be reflected in almost all the aspects of daily life, especially in the meals: chopsticks are round; bowls are round and even the table is round.

Since the ancient times, Chinese have been using the round table for dinner while the square table for sacrifice. *Yuan* symbolizes auspiciousness, so round table represents reunion, harmony and happiness. Therefore, in China, the round table is always a top choice in an important banquet or family reunion dinner.

A typical round table in Chinese families

1. Chinese Banquet

1.1 Seating

Seating should be appropriately arranged before dinners according to the guests' number, seniority and organizational hierarchy. Rules could be slightly adjusted to different situations, but never forget a golden rule—the host leader takes the seat facing the door and leaders of both sides should sit next to each other. (主人上座为对门之座，主与宾相邻而坐)

1.1.1 Guest seating

The seating rules will be different when one or two chief hosts attend the dinner. The following examples will reveal more details.

1) In a situation of one chief host present (H: host, G: guest)

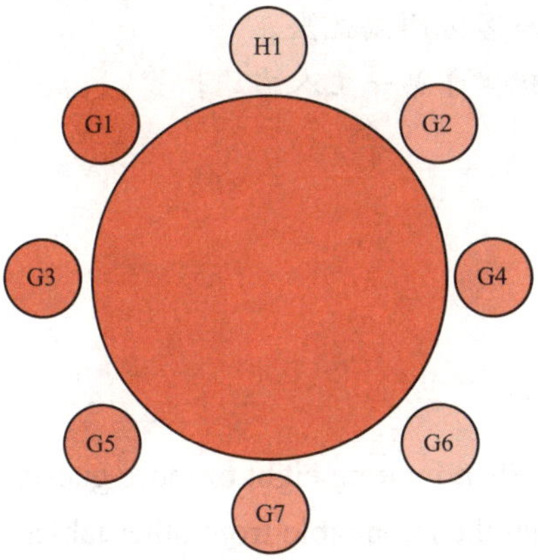

Entrance of the room

排座原则：

- 主宾（G1）和第二主宾（G2）分别就坐于第一主人（H1）的右边和左边。其余宾客以此类推。
- 主人（H1）面向餐厅正门。

2) In a situation of two chief hosts present (H: host, G: guest)

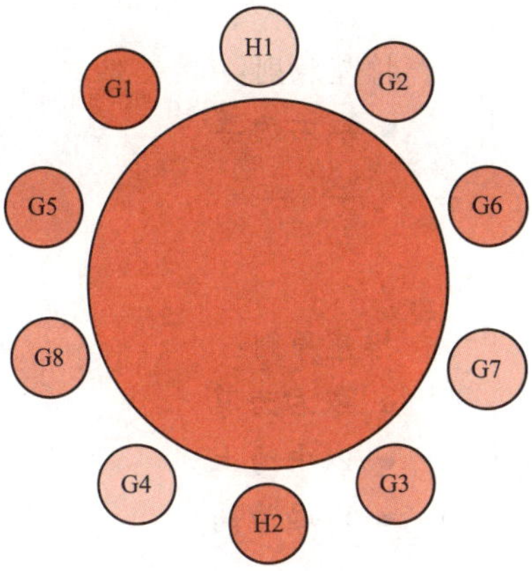

Entrance of the room

图一

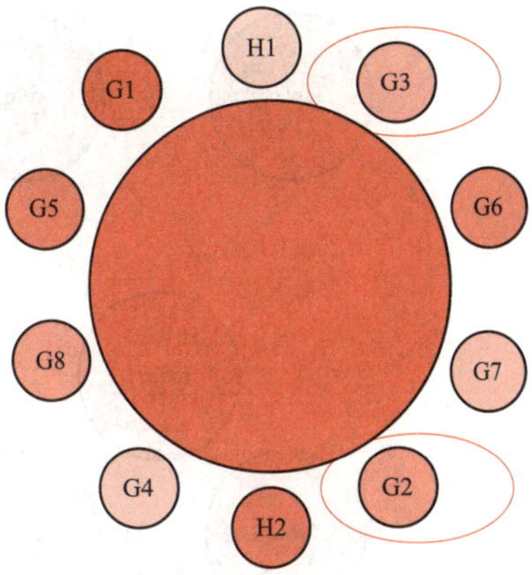

Entrance of the room

图二

排座原则：
- 第一主人面向餐厅正门。
- 两位主人（H1 & H2）面对面就坐。
- 第一主宾（G1）和第二主宾（G2）分别就坐于第一主人（H1）的右边和左边。第三主宾（G3）和第四主宾（G4）分别就坐于第二主人（H2）的右边和左边。（如图一）
- 如两位主人的地位几乎相当，则可以采用图二的排座方法。

3) With the same number of hosts and guests (H: host, G: guest)

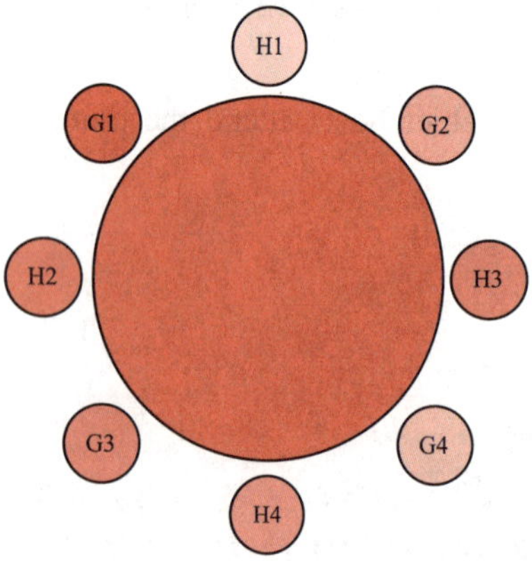

Entrance of the room

排座原则：
- 第一主人面向餐厅正门。
- 主方与客方间隔就坐。
- 主宾就坐于第一主人右边。

1.1.2 Dinner tables arrangement

Generally speaking, a table has eight to ten seats. When inviting eight or more guests, it is best to arrange two or more tables and clearly distinguish the main table from other tables. The following are rules of table arrangements. Table 1 is the head table.

For example:

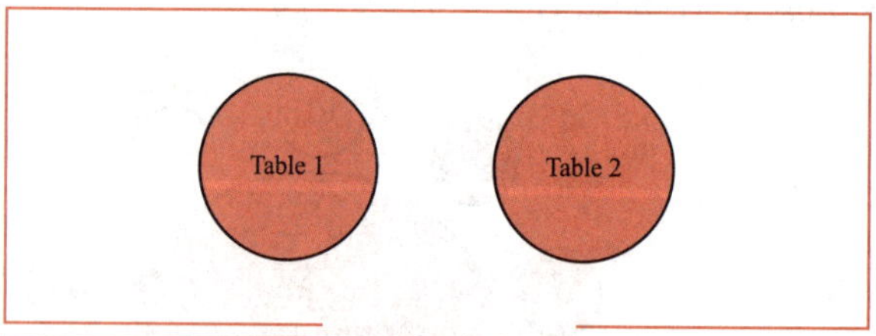

排座原则：
- 以右为尊

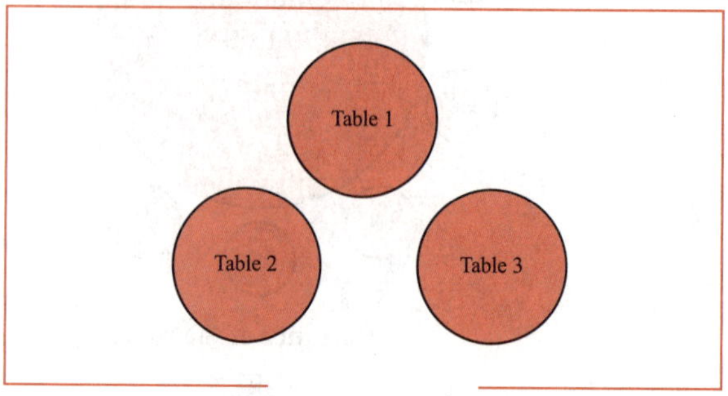

排座原则：
- 以右为尊
- 以中为上
- 以远为高

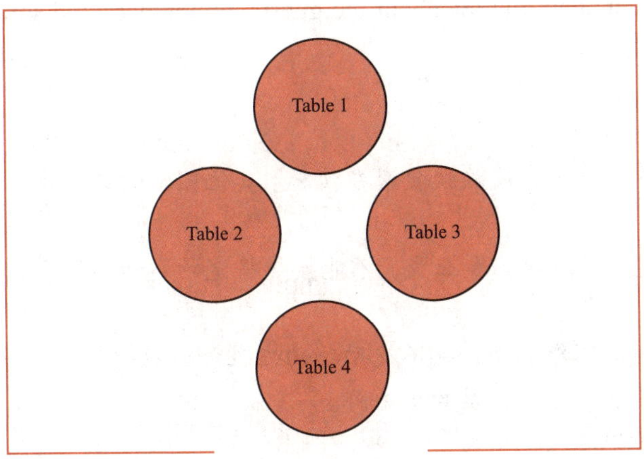

排座原则：
- 以右为尊
- 以远为高

1.2 Table etiquette

1.2.1 Before the dinner

1) Invitation

Dinner invitation should be sent at least a day before the dinner, so the guests could make a schedule. Actually, in both Chinese and Western cultures, being invited is often considered an honor and respect.

中国四大名著之一《西游记》中，孙悟空因为没有受邀蟠桃盛会而大闹天宫。

希腊神话里，不和女神厄里斯因为没有受邀阿喀琉斯父母的婚礼而投下了“不和的金苹果”。

A quick response is required upon receiving the invitation.

2) Arrival

Chinese people usually arrive at the dinner 10-20 minutes later than the appointed time. But the delayed time should not be more than 20 minutes, which is considered to be rude and disrespectful to the host.

Arriving at the dinner, the first thing one should do is to greet the host and “guest of honor”. However, don’t forget to communicate with other guests.

3) Seating

The seating order is very important. According to Chinese tradition, the elders and the honored guests should be seated first; otherwise, it will be regarded as rudeness.

In modern society, especially in Western culture where the etiquette of “lady first” is highly valued, ladies are the first to be seated and gentlemen are supposed to pull the chairs for them.

Being right or left is also important. In a business dinner, it is common to get seated from the left-hand side of the chair and leaving the table on the right.

4) Ordering dishes

The host should order dishes for the guests. However, if only one or two guests are invited, it is acceptable for the guests to order food in person.

With different food culture, the host should know about the guests' preferences and some taboos on food in advance.

中国人的饮食禁忌相对较少，一些少数民族饮食存在禁忌。其他国家的文化存在各种不尽相同的禁忌。如：

* 西方人多不喜欢吃动物的头、尾、足、内脏和血液，不能接受将宠物类动物作为食物的行为。
* 穆斯林的教义规定不可以吃猪肉，不能喝酒，也不吃动物的内脏和血液。
* 日本人和韩国人喜欢少油清淡的烹调方法，喜欢吃海鲜。
* 印度人把牛视为神，切不可邀请印度人吃牛肉。

Do not go over the budget, or you have to pay for the overrun.

In a Chinese banquet, the number of dishes usually goes with the number of diners. The courses should include the cold dishes as well as the hot dishes, such as soup, meat, vegetables, entrée, fruits, beverage and so on.

Restaurants with local characteristics are also advisable, and dishes with local flavor may impress the guests deeply.

1.2.2 Table manners

1) Wine culture

a. The origin of wine

China is one of the countries with the longest history of wine making in the world, and wine has a history of thousands of years in China, forming a unique wine culture.

《诗经》记载："十月获稻，为此春酒"，表明当时中国酒之兴起，至今已有 5000 年的历史了。

There are different opinions about the origin of wine. The following are three common explanations that people generally agree on.

猿猴造酒：古猿将吃不完的果实藏起来，久而久之，果实腐烂，野果通过自然发酵而生成酒浆，因而有"尝于石岩深处得猿酒"的传说。

仪狄造酒：从前，舜的女儿仪狄擅长酿酒，仪狄把酒献给了禹，他喝了之后觉得芳香四溢，但就此疏远了仪狄，戒绝了美酒。

杜康造酒：曹操的《短歌行》中提到"何以解忧，唯有杜康"。制酒业封杜康为祖师爷，而杜康也成了酒的代名词。

b. The characteristics of wine

Chinese wine culture is Chinese liquor (*Baijiu*) culture. Chinese liquor is one of the six most famous distilled spirits in the world, and one of the finest liquor in China is Maotai (茅台). Chinese liquor has a unique style among all the alcoholic beverages. Compared with other liquor, Chinese liquor has a special and incomparable flavor. The color is white crystal and colorless transparent; the smell is pleasant and pure; the taste is soft, sweet and clear. Just a sip of Chinese liquor can give people a great sense of joy and happiness.

For Western wine, there are some familiar names, such as brandy, whiskey, wine, champagne, cocktail, etc.

Brandy (白兰地)：是指葡萄发酵后经蒸馏而得到的高度酒精，再经橡木桶贮存而成的酒。通常被人称为“葡萄酒的灵魂”。

Whiskey (威士忌)：是一种由大麦等谷物酿制，在橡木桶中陈酿多年后，调配成 43 度左右的烈性蒸馏酒。英国人称之为“生命之水”。按产地分为苏格兰威士忌、爱尔兰威士忌、美国威士忌和加拿大威士忌。

Wine (葡萄酒)：泛指葡萄酒、红酒、白葡萄酒。

Champagne (香槟)：香槟是指生产于法国香槟区的符合一系列特殊标准的葡萄酒。

Cocktail (鸡尾酒)：是一种混合饮品，通常以朗姆酒、金酒、龙舌兰、伏特加、威士忌、白兰地等烈酒或葡萄酒作为基酒，再配以果汁、蛋清、苦精、牛奶、咖啡、糖等其他辅助材料。

c. Wine virtue

Historically, Confucianism was held up as an orthodoxy for governing the state. The custom of wine is also influenced by the Confucian wine culture. Confucianism emphasizes wine virtue. The meaning of wine virtue is that drinking should be virtuous, and cannot be as decadent as King Zhou (纣王) in wine. Confucianism does not oppose drinking wine, which is a virtue to worship God, support the elderly and serve guests.

儒家提倡**“德将无醉”**

d. Etiquette in wine

Drinking is one of the ways to show the hosts' hospitality in China. Beverages such as liquors, Western-style wine, and beer can be seen on the table.

—Etiquette in wine pouring

Conventionally speaking, the host or waiter pour wine to guests. Guests should raise their glasses to thank the host. While pouring wine, the host should pay attention to the following three rules.

1. 对客人一视同仁，不能只为个别人斟酒。
2. 注意顺序，以自己为起点按照顺时针方向斟酒，也可以先为尊长斟酒。
3. 斟酒需适量，白酒一般倒八分满至九分满。

The amount varies in different liquors. While the glasses for *Baijiu* should be filled to 80%–90% of the capacity, 30% of the capacity would be appropriate for red wine glasses.

人们使用高脚红酒杯饮用红酒。西方人将喝红酒视为一种享受的过程，因此对红酒的色泽、香味、口感等方面的感受尤为看重。

红酒对温度的要求比较严格，所以喝红酒使用高脚杯，是为了避免人的手温在握住杯体的时候影响红酒的品质。而平时我们经常看见人们喝红酒前会轻轻摇晃酒杯，其实是为了欣赏和观察红酒沿着杯子流淌时体现出来的色泽，因此倒红酒时不应倒满。

—Etiquette in wine toasting

Toasting is an essential part of a banquet. As the dinner starts, the host makes a toast to the guests to welcome them. At the end of the dinner, the guests will toast the host as a form of appreciation. The following are some rules for toasting.

敬酒时间：通常由主人先发起敬酒。如果致正式祝酒词，应在特定时间进行，例如，宾主入座后、用餐前，或者吃过主菜后、甜品上桌前。

敬酒顺序：一般情况下，敬酒应以年龄大小、职位高低、宾主身份为先后顺序。如果没有特殊人物在场，碰酒最好按顺时针顺序，不要厚此薄彼。

敬酒姿势：起身站立，右手端起酒杯，再以左手托付杯底，面带微笑，目视祝酒对象，同时要说祝福的话。

敬酒仪态：碰杯时，应让自己的酒杯低于对方的酒杯，表示尊敬；当碰杯距离较远时，用杯底轻碰桌面，表示碰杯。

In China, people used to persuade others to drink as much as possible, which was considered as hospitality. But now, more and more people show their dislike to this custom, as they believe that it is disrespectful to force others to drink. Therefore, toasts should not be excessive and drinking should be moderate.

2) Utensils

There are some rules on the use of utensils like bowls, chopsticks, plates, and cups on the dinner table, which is still followed up as traditions till now.

Note 1: In China, it is a polite table manner to hold the bowl when eating. But in the Republic of Korea, it is not proper to do so.

Note 2: Use the chopsticks appropriately.

握筷禁忌：

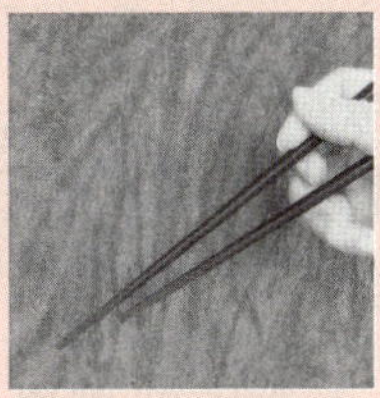

1. 三长两短
（握筷时筷子长短不齐）

2. 击盏敲盅
（用筷子敲击饭碗）

3. 当众上香
（筷子垂直插在米饭中）

4. 仙人指路
（握筷时食指伸出）

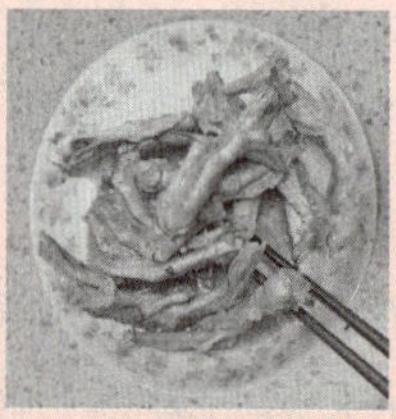

5. 迷箸刨坟
（用筷子翻动碟中的菜品）

6. 颠倒乾坤
（将筷子颠倒使用）

7. 品箸留声
（嘬吸筷子并发出声音）

8. 泪箸遗珠
（夹菜时菜汁流落在桌面）

9. 定海神针
（取菜时用筷子插食物）

Note 3: When serving yourself with dishes, it is recommended to use a spoon or bowl so as to avoid the broth falling on the table.

Note 4: During the meal, it is not appropriate to rotate the lazy susan (餐桌转盘) when someone else is serving himself from the main bowl. While rotating the lazy susan, make sure that it doesn't hit any utensils around.

Note 5: For the sake of food hygiene, serving spoons and chopsticks (公勺和公筷) should be used when serving oneself from the main bowls.

2. Western Banquet

2.1 Seating arrangement

Different from round tables in Chinese dinner, square tables are usually used in Western dinners. The rule of seating etiquette is the arrangement that men and women are cross-seated, with an aim of social interactions.

Two examples will be given.

a. Head seats on the same side with guest seats (Ht: host, Hs: hostess, F: female guest, M: male guest)

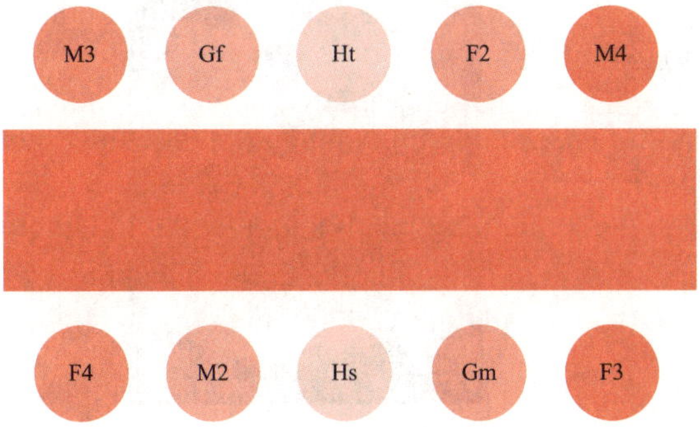

排座原则：以右为尊、异性相邻

b. Head seats at the ends of the table

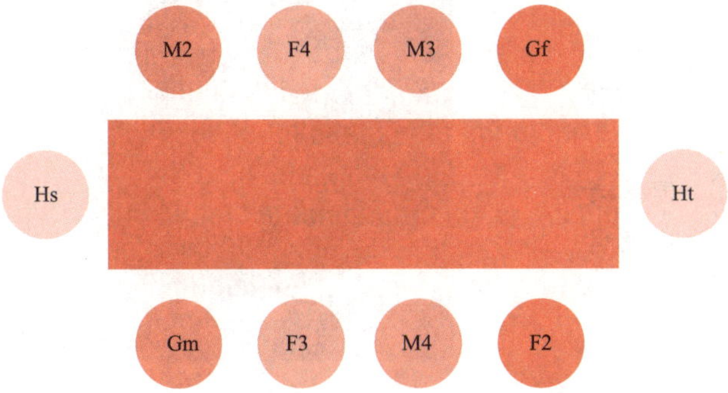

排座原则：
以右为尊、异性相邻

2.2 Western-style courses

Unlike Chinese dinner, where guests sit around the table and share main bowl on the table, the food in Western meal is brought to each diner one by one during the dinner. Food is served at the table in order, and the previous dish will be removed upon the service of the next dish. The order should not be disrupted.

Traditional Western-style food includes appetizers, soup, entrée (white meat), main dishes (red meat), salad, desserts, and beverages.

- 开胃菜（头盘）一般品质较高，但量比较少。如鱼子酱，鹅肝酱，法式焗蜗牛等。通常为带咸味或酸味的菜品。

温煮蛋配鱼子酱

- 西式汤分为清汤和浓汤。
- 清汤通常有牛肉清汤、蔬菜汤、鸡肉清汤等。
- 浓汤则有奶油蘑菇汤、南瓜浓汤、土豆浓汤等。

奶油蘑菇汤

- 白肉包括海鲜和禽肉（鸡肉）。因其煮熟后肉呈白色，称为白肉。白肉脂肪较少。一般配以白葡萄酒。
- 红肉包括猪肉、牛肉、羊肉。因其煮熟后肉呈红色，称为红肉。红肉通常脂肪较多。一般配以红酒。

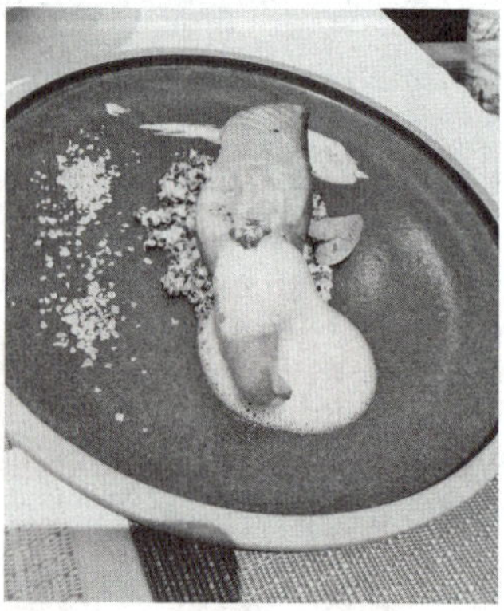

鱼肉

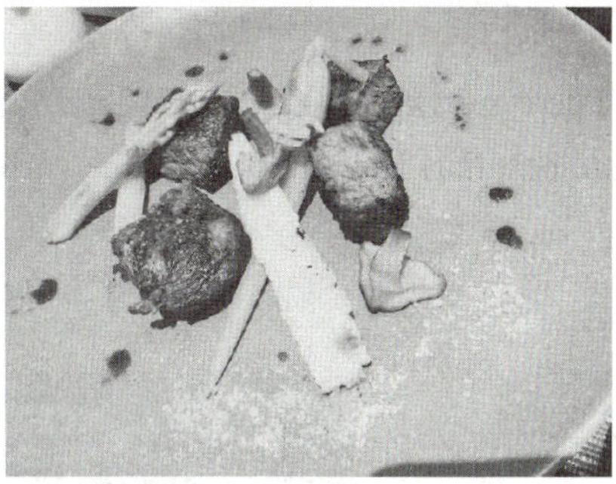

牛排

- 沙拉的原料很多，蔬菜、肉类、禽蛋等食材煮熟凉透后或直接以生料加入各种调味酱做成。味道清爽，解腻开胃。沙拉可以作为头盘或者主菜后蔬菜出现。

蔬菜沙拉

- 西餐甜点的种类繁多，一般有蛋糕、饼干、布丁、慕斯、冰淇淋等。

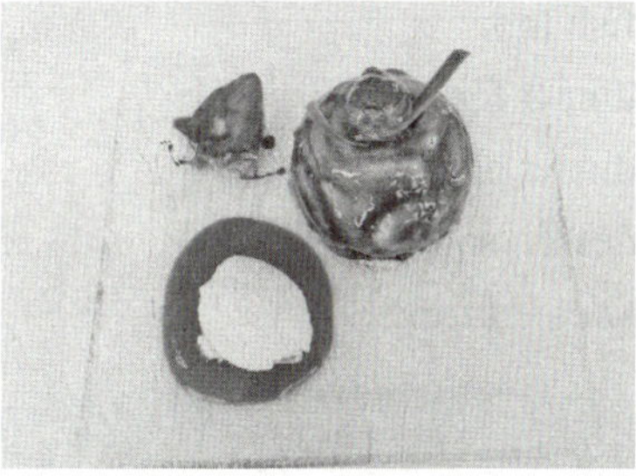

草莓冰淇淋

- 餐后的饮品一般是不含酒精的。如茶、咖啡、果汁等。

咖啡

2.3 Utensils

There are various kinds of Western utensils in Western dinner and the order of using them is more peculiar. The number and the variety needed are different in different levels of dinner.

1. butter knife
2. bread plate
3. coffee cup
4. napkin
5. appetizer fork
6. fish fork
7. dinner fork
8. dinner plate
9. dessert spoon
10. dessert fork
11. water glass
12. red wine goblet
13. white wine goblet
14. champagne goblet
15. dinner knife
16. fish knife
17. appetizer knife
18. dinner spoon
19. soup spoon

酒杯是西餐中重要的餐具之一。酒杯分为很多种，形状和用途各不相同。常见的有：

红酒杯

香槟杯

白兰地杯

2.4 Napkin

There is an old saying that goes "the very first thing you do when you take your seat at the dining table is thinking about your napkin." Using the napkin appropriately and elegantly helps you deal with all kinds of Western dinners with ease. Usually, the napkin is placed on the dinner plate, or in a cup.

据说在十五六世纪的英国，由于没有剃刀，男士们都留着大胡子。当时还没有刀叉，就餐时大胡子很容易沾上油或汤汁。因此，家庭主妇们就给男士们配备用于清洁嘴巴的方巾。这是餐巾由来的其中一种说法。

2.4.1 Functions of a napkin

One function of using a napkin is to avoid broth or soup falling directly on your clothes; the other is to clean your mouth, especially when you finish the meal or before you talk to other people. But napkins are not used for cleaning the utensils, hands, or face. When napkins are provided, do not use paper tissues.

2.4.2 Using napkins

After you take the seat, you should wait for your host and hostess to take their napkins from the table before taking yours. Don't dig in until it is indicated by the host. Unless you are a child or disabled person, napkins should not be hung in front of your breast, but placed on your laps.

If you have to leave in the middle of the dinner, the napkin should be placed on the chair. After the dinner is finished, the napkin should be folded with ease and put on the left side of the plate on the table.

2.5 Table etiquette

1) Westerners follow the rule of "Lady First". In a formal dinner, gentlemen usually show their respect for ladies.

2) Pay attention to your sitting posture. The "elbows off the table" rule applies only when you are actually eating, while "elbows on the table" is acceptable between the courses when people are talking.

3) In a formal dinner, do not wipe or clean the utensils. Chinese people tend to clean the utensils with tea or drinking water, but in a formal dinner, this means that you worry about the sanitation of the dinning environment.

4) Do not point your utensils to others when talking to them, which is regarded as offensive and provocative. Do not lick or suck the utensils, as it is an implication of flirting.

5) The placement of utensils reflects different meanings. The mistake in placing utensils may result in misunderstanding to restaurant staff, and then the dishes you like will be removed.

(paused)

(finished)

6) You will be asked "How would you like your steak done?" when you are ordering. The correct answer should be: **rare, medium rare, medium, medium well, well done**.

7) Such courses as pork chop, steak and lamb require different ways of eating. In the British way, people have a bite of meat after the one cut, while in American style, people tend to enjoy the dish after they cut the meat into smaller pieces.

8) When cutting steak, the fork on the left hand presses the steak and the knife on the right cuts the steak, usually from the left to the right. Cut the steak into bite-size pieces that you can chew and swallow easily.

9) Do not slurp when you are drinking soup, liquor, or beverage. Instead, sip it slowly and silently.

2.6 Handling of special cases

1) How to deal with the situation of getting food stuck between teeth?

If you have food stuck between your teeth, do not clean it up in public. Please go to the bathroom.

2) How to deal with the situation of spilling something on the table?

If there is a spill on the table, ask the waiter to clean up your mess.

3) How to deal with the situation of dropping knife and fork on the floor?

When you're eating, the knife and fork accidentally fall onto the floor. Don't bend down to pick it up. You can signal the waiter to handle it and replace the new tableware.

4) How to do if you're left-handed?

The tableware cannot be changed casually. If you are left-handed, use the knife and fork interchangeably. But at the end of the meal, make sure to place them as the right-handed person would use it.

II. Buffet 自助餐

Contents:

1. Dishes served in a buffet
2. Etiquette in a buffet

Buffet is an informal Western type of meal in international business field. It is a system of serving meals in which food is placed in a public area where the diners generally serve themselves. Hot dishes as well as cold dishes are offered, while the cold dishes are usually the majority, so it is also called "cold buffet".

Buffet is a widely accepted type of meal in business activities, because it caters to the different preferences of different people, especially when it is a grand business meal in which there are a great number of diners.

自助餐这种就餐形式起源于公元8～11世纪北欧的“斯堪的纳维亚式餐前冷食”和“亨联早餐(Hunt breakfast)”。在20世纪30年代传入中国。

自助餐分为设座和无设座两种，即是否为客人提供座位。

在无设座自助餐厅中，通常会提供齐腰高的小桌子，方便客人就餐。侍应会手托饮料酒水穿梭于客人之中，客人可自由选用。

1. Dishes Served in a Buffet

As it is mentioned, there is a wide range of cold dishes in a buffet. A high-class buffet serves only some kinds of hot dishes, including the barbecued or roasted ones, usually made by the chef on site to ensure their wonderful tastes.

Dishes displayed in a buffet include:
Cold dishes: sea food, appetizer, etc.
Soup: western light soup and thick soup
Hot dishes: steak, pork, mutton, chicken, duck, etc.
Vegetables: raw or cooked, or made into salad
Dessert: cake, cookies, budding, pie, ice cream, etc.
Drink: wine, juice, coffee, punch, etc.
Fruit: strawberry, orange, melon, cherry, etc.

海鲜类冷菜

肉禽类热菜

汤

甜点

沙拉

水果

饮料

2. Etiquette in a Buffet

2.1 Take a look

Before you start the food trip, you'd better take a look at all the dishes served so as to choose the best ones you like. This is a step usually missed by many people.

2.2 Follow the rules

You'd better follow the rules in taking dishes in the suggested order, cold dishes first, then soup, hot dishes, dessert, fruit and drink at last.

2.3 Good manners

1) Line up and wait for your turn when picking up the dishes, and leave the line at once after finishing.

2) Don't pile the dishes up on the plate. Although buffets are "all-you-can-eat" style, it is suggested to take small amounts of food of no more than three dishes at a time, and return for more servings if desired. This will help to avoid wasting food, especially when the dish is not to your taste.

3) You don't have to fetch food for others. An essential feature of a buffet is that the diners serve themselves, which may be obstructed if you insist on fetching food for others. And it will bring embarrassment if the food is not favorable.

4) It is forbidden to take the food out of the restaurant in a buffet, no matter how delicious it is.

5) It is usually suggested to clean the table after finishing the meal.

III. Working Lunch 工作餐

Contents:

1. What is a working lunch?
2. Etiquette in a working lunch

1. What Is a Working Lunch?

A working lunch refers to an informal business meal which is of a relaxed style. There are two different ways of having working lunch— one is a quick lunch provided by the company; the other is a table lunch in a restaurant with some colleagues.

Here the etiquette of table meals when having a working lunch in a restaurant will be mainly discussed. As an informal meal with colleagues, it is not totally for the purpose of feeding oneself. Instead, while having lunch, the diners also chat to exchange information, discuss business projects and so on. That's why a working lunch is also defined as a business meal.

工作餐既不同于正式宴会，也不同于亲友聚会，正式程度介乎两者之间。工作餐不强调形式和规格，重在创造一种氛围，主要目的是更好地利用就餐时间和聚餐的机会进行更多的商务接触，或者是同事之间借就餐的场合进行会议商讨。工作餐通常安排在日间进行，所以也叫工作午餐。

2. Etiquette in a Working Lunch

A working lunch is comparatively casual if it is a meal with colleagues. If a boss or a business partner is invited, more manners are required.

2.1 As the host of a working lunch, it is necessary to get everything ready.

1) Purpose

明确就餐目的，不应该无的放矢。

2) People invited

明确参与就餐的人员。一般来说，工作聚餐的人数不宜过多，十人以内较为合适。除了人数，还要确定人员名单，并逐一通知。

3) Time

确定时间。一般选择工作日的午间，而不是节假日。就餐时间不宜过长，一小时左右比较合适。

4) Place

确定地点。由于时间有限，工作餐不宜选择过于偏远的就餐场所，以免浪费往返的时间。最好选择比较安静、环境优雅的餐厅，以便商谈商务事宜，并提前订座。

5) The bill

负责最后结账。如果是熟悉的同事之间，也可以商定各自付费的原则。

6) Seating	不需安排座次，就餐时可自由就座。
7) Dishes	确定就餐形式。工作餐的菜肴以简单为主，最好采用“分餐制”的就餐方式。

2.2　As a person invited, you should

1) respond to the invitation without delay.

2) join the working lunch on time, because the time for it is quite limited and lateness means wasting the time for the meal and discussion.

3) focus on the topic. Don’t drift off.

无论是发起人还是参与者，工作餐都不宜携带烟酒，特别是烈酒，也不应该拍照、录像等，更不应该将其上传至社交网站或发布于朋友圈等。

2.3　The principle of tipping

- 如果是堂食，在上菜时要给一定的小费，一般来说，午餐的小费是账单的 10%到 15%，晚餐则是 15%到 20%；
- 如果打包带走，可以给小费也可以不给；
- 在麦当劳、肯德基等快餐店就餐时则不用付小费。

Exercise 章节练习

Discussion:

1. Scan the QR code to watch the video, and try to find out the rude behaviors in dining.

2. Read the poem *Invitation to Wine* (Li Bai, translated by Xu Yuanchong), and then discuss the following questions with your group members.

Invitation to Wine

Li Bai

Tr. Xu Yuanchong

Do you not see the Yellow River come from the sky,
Rushing into the sea and ne'er come back?
Do you not see the mirrors bright in chambers high
Grieve o'er your snow-white hair though once it was silk-black?
When hopes are won, oh! Drink your fill in high delight,
And never leave your wine-cup empty in moonlight!
Heaven has made us talents, we're not made in vain.
A thousand gold coins spent, more will turn up again.
Kill a cow, cook a sheep and let us merry be,
And drink three hundred cupfuls of wine in high glee!
Dear friends of mine,
Cheer up, cheer up!
I invite you to wine.
Do not put down your cup!

1) Talk about your understanding about “劝酒” (invite or urge sb. to drink) in Chinese wine culture.

2) Some people say that Chinese wine culture cannot be separated from the poetry, so try to find other Chinese poems about wine and then discuss the significance of the combination of Chinese poetry and wine culture.

Module Four
Etiquette in the Workplace
职场礼仪

Chapter One

Etiquette in Job Interview

面试礼仪

学习任务

1. 了解面试前应做的准备工作。
2. 了解面试过程中的礼仪要求。
3. 了解面试结束后应该做的事情。

Warm-up:

Who do you think will receive the offer of employment at last?

Case

Who Will Receive the Offer of Employment?

Hanna, Jaden and Miranda are going to graduate from college and are applying for the post of manager assistant in a foreign-capital enterprise. At the end of the interview, the interviewer brought a question which is commonly seen in interviews: "Do you have any other questions to ask?"

Hanna replied: "I would like to know what countermeasures the board of directors will adopt to resolve the problem brought by the failure in attracting public concern in the new product release last month?"

After thinking for a while, Jaden replied that he had no more questions to ask.

Miranda asked: "What are the standards of the company in assessing the performance of the employees?"

I. Before the Interview 面试前

Contents:

1. The research
2. The paper work
3. The mock interview
4. Dress

1. The Research

1.1 The research on the company

Obtain some basic information of the company you are applying for. If you are familiar with the company's history, development, operation, management, personnel structure and so on, you won't be embarrassed in answering the relative questions from the interviewer.

1.2 The clear understanding to your target position

Before the interview, you'd better get familiarized with the post you are applying for. You are likely to win the interviewer's favor if you know well about the duty of the post and the skills required.

2. The Paper Work

Have all the paper copies of the materials you need ready before you set out. For example:

Application Letter

July 25th, 2018
Dear Mr. Green,

I am writing to apply for the post of HR manager assistant as I have learned it from the advertisement in Global Times.

I graduated from Guangxi University in 2018, majoring in secretary. I have strong interest in this field and want to begin my career in your company. I would be very grateful if you offer me a change to have an interview.

I am looking forward to meeting you.

Yours sincerely,

Sally Peng

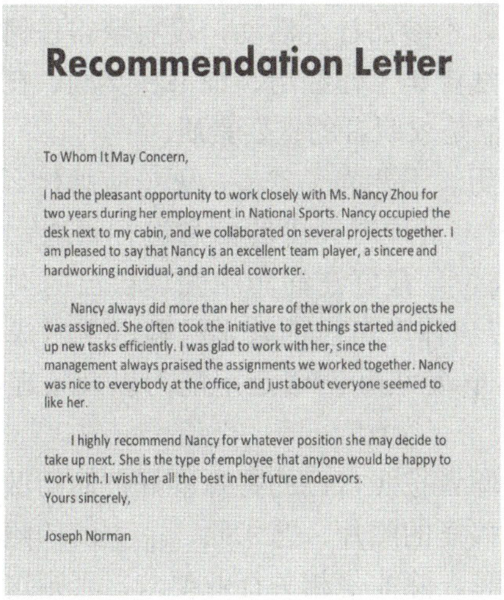

Recommendation Letter

To Whom It May Concern,

I had the pleasant opportunity to work closely with Ms. Nancy Zhou for two years during her employment in National Sports. Nancy occupied the desk next to my cabin, and we collaborated on several projects together. I am pleased to say that Nancy is an excellent team player, a sincere and hardworking individual, and an ideal coworker.

Nancy always did more than her share of the work on the projects he was assigned. She often took the initiative to get things started and picked up new tasks efficiently. I was glad to work with her, since the management always praised the assignments we worked together. Nancy was nice to everybody at the office, and just about everyone seemed to like her.

I highly recommend Nancy for whatever position she may decide to take up next. She is the type of employee that anyone would be happy to work with. I wish her all the best in her future endeavors.

Yours sincerely,

Joseph Norman

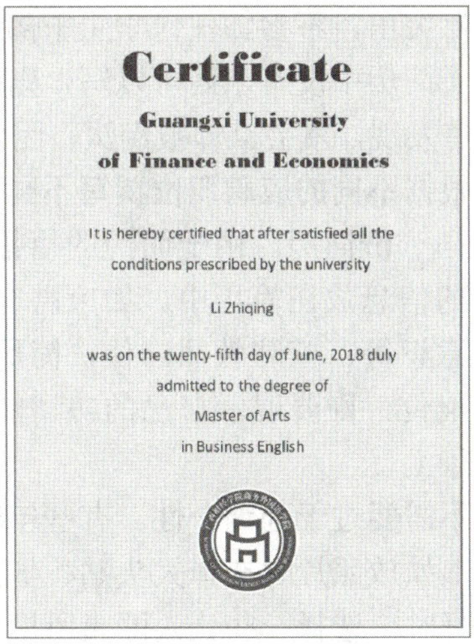

Certificate

Guangxi University of Finance and Economics

It is hereby certified that after satisfied all the conditions prescribed by the university

Li Zhiqing

was on the twenty-fifth day of June, 2018 duly admitted to the degree of

Master of Arts

in Business English

简历的撰写

1. 简历一般包括个人信息、学历背景、工作经历、获奖情况与证书等几个部分。

（1）个人信息：包括姓名（如有英文名，可以同时列出）、性别、出生日期、婚姻状况、毕业院校及专业、联系方式、求职意向、兴趣爱好等。

（2）学历背景：中文简历一般从过去的学习经历开始写，而英文简历则从最近的学习经历开始写。建议列出 2～3 条学历背景即可，如博士—硕士—学士，学士—高中，不需要把小学甚至幼儿园的学习经历列出。

（3）工作经历：对于有社会工作经历的求职者来说，重点列出就职单位、岗位、主要职责（如曾经负责或参与大型项目）。对于应届毕业生来说，主要介绍自己在校的学生干部工作经历、兼职和社会活动经历（如志愿者活动、游学、企业实习等）。

（4）获奖情况与证书：获奖奖项一般从等级高的奖项开始写（如国际奖—国家奖—省部级奖—市级奖—校级奖），但不需要列多于 5 项。如果证书数量比较多，则主要列出与专业或求职职位相关的即可。

2. 简历撰写的要求

（1）简洁。很多大学毕业生以为，把自己所有的辉煌成就全部放在简历中，会帮助自己在众多求职者中脱颖而出。但事实是，招聘单位并不会有太多时间用于阅读求职者的简历，如果简历太繁杂，招聘者只会失去耐心，放弃该求职者。因此，简历最好不要超过两页，每项不多于五个点，每点不多于两行。

（2）排版一目了然。将简历中的几大部分分类，突出显示大标题和重要的信息。将重要信息放在首页。

（3）无错误。简历写好后要仔细检查校对，必须做到无文字错误、无信息错误、用词准确。

3. 几点建议

（1）不夸大、不造假。简历中提供的信息应该实事求是。有些大学毕业生在求学期间成绩不够突出，不参加任何学生干部工作，不参加社会活动，没有获得任何证书和奖励，以至于简历中没有东西可以写，则想办法虚构工作经历、证书和奖励。在面试中如果被面试官发现，就会立即被淘汰，因为诚信是求职者的重要素质。

（2）根据不同的应聘职位撰写不同的简历。不要为了省事，无论应聘什么公司什么职位都用同一份简历。由于简历的篇幅有限，必须对列出的信息进行筛选，选择对该职位有用的信息放在简历中。如应聘客服岗位，最好在简历中强调自己的沟通能力和团队合作意识等；应聘教师岗位，简历中应该体现自己的教学经验、学术成就；应聘行政助理岗位，则要展示自己的协调能力，计算机和网络运用能力以及条理清晰的思维逻辑。

（3）不需要过于强调个性。有些年轻求职者按照自己的特殊喜好把简历做成很有个性的风格。如放照片时选择大头贴、生活中搞怪的照片、艺术照、非主流的照片等；在写兴趣爱好时，选择一些让人匪夷所思的信息。除非是相关行业要求，否则这些兴趣爱好对你应聘的工作并没有帮助，反而让招聘者觉得你不靠谱。

3. The Mock Interview

3.1 Questions expected

It is suggested that you prepare for some questions which may be arranged for your interview, especially for some professional posts, which require specific skills and specialized knowledge. And you may face questions about professional fields or you may be asked to carry out an on-the-site operation to test whether you are the right person for the post. Therefore, please have a revision on the professional knowledge and practical skills probably necessary for the post.

Furthermore, get ready to answer other common questions in interviews, such as the ones about self-introduction, salary expectations, the reason of choosing that post in that company, the future plans in career development, etc.

3.2 Questions ready to ask

Interview is a bi-directional communication, in which you may also ask for the information you want to know. But you need to sort out most of the questions you are going to ask before you go to the interview rather than think of all the questions in a haste during the interview. In this way, you will not miss anything you want to know, and may successfully impress the interviewer as a person who plans things well.

But you have to eliminate the questions irrelevant. Don't show too much concern to the problems unrelated to the job or to the things beyond your purview. Don't emphasize too much on your self-interest. Never ask questions about the information or issues having been released in the recruitment notice or other documents.

3.3 Practice

If you are a newbie in the interview, you'd better rehearse before the interview. Ask some friends or classmates to play the roles of interviewers and you try to be the interviewee, which will help you get experienced, more or less, and confident enough to face the fierce challenge.

4. Dress

Choose the proper dress for the interview and get all the stuff ready the night before the interview.

You have to know that different dresses are for different posts. For example:

- **An image of capability and tact for the post of management**

- **An image of amiability and carefulness for the post of secretary or assistant**

- **An image of elegance and learnedness for the post of teacher**

- **An image of uniqueness and stylishness for the post of designer**

Dress is not the only thing you have to get prepared. Choose a bag or briefcase for this occasion, and put all the stuff you need for the interview into it. Have the shoes polished before it is too late.

Your hair should be clean and neat to make you look energetic. A light makeup is appropriate for ladies.

除了以上几点，还要再次确认面试的时间和地点，了解清楚交通路线以及所用的时间。提前十分钟左右到达现场。

特别是对于应届毕业生来说，切勿和父母或亲戚一同前往面试现场，会给人一种过于依赖、缺乏独立能力的印象。

II. During the Interview 面试时

Contents:

1. Dos
2. Don'ts

Dos:

1. Keep quiet when you are waiting for your turn to be interviewed. Don't walk around or accost other candidates. This is good for you to calm down before the interview.
2. Knock on the door before you enter the interview room.
3. Sit properly and speak loud enough.
4. Be energetic and relaxed.
5. Stay confident and composed when answering questions.
6. Go straight to the point to make your answer concise and clear.
7. Show your appreciation and leave politely when the interview comes to an end.

Don'ts:

1. Don't be cocky or slippery.
2. The interviewer is usually disgusted with the person who greases the wheels or emphasizes his social connections.
3. Never try to perfect yourself by telling others off, no matter whether it is on purpose or not.
4. Don't put the one about salary on the top of your question list to the interviewer, or else you will come across as a person who receives rather than gives.
5. When the interview is over, don't go back into the interview room to ask another question which suddenly comes into your mind.

Please watch the video and try to remember the etiquette in a job interview.

III. After the Interview 面试后

Contents:

What should be done after the interview?

Learn to appreciate no matter whether you are employed or not. You may have many ways to show your appreciation, such as telephone, e-mail or letter of thanks.

Keep the thank-you call short, preferably no more than two minutes.

Keep your thank-you letter brief, preferably no longer than one page. The main purpose of the letter is to briefly introduce yourself, mention the interview time and thank the recruiter, reiterate your interest in the company and the position, and express your confidence. You can also provide additional materials to prove that you can contribute to the company.

Be patient for the announcement of the result if it is not released at once after the interview. A three or five-day wait is reasonable, so don't bother to ask about the final result.

In general, if you have not received a reply two weeks after the interview or by the time the interviewer promised to notify the applicant, you should write or call the recruiter or the interviewer to ask if a decision has been made.

You'd better have another string to your bow, because it is common to be eliminated in an interview. Pull yourself up and get ready for another interview.

Exercise 章节练习

1. Simulation scenario of a job interview:

1) All students are to work in two teams. The first team is divided into groups of three or four students, who play the roles of the interviewers in a company. The interviewers should offer a job advertisement to show relative details about the company, including the name of the firm, the post offered and the requirements, etc. Before the interview, the interviewers have to

decide what questions to ask.

2) The second team are the interviewees. They can choose the company and the post they like and go for a face-to-face interview. Before the interview, the interviewees should get all the materials needed ready. The etiquette in a job interview should always be remembered.

3) When the first round of interview is over, start a second round, with the roles exchanged.

4) The teacher comments on the performance.

2. Case study

Directions: Discuss the cases in groups and make analysis of them:

Case 1: Zhang Lili, a finance major, was happy and nervous when she received an interview notice from a well-known enterprise. The interview was smooth and the interviewer was pleased with her. But in the end, the interviewer asked: "Based on your personality traits, we want to arrange you in the office, which may not be in line with your major. What do you think?" Zhang Lili didn't make up her mind and said, "Or I'll talk to my parents." As a result, the interviewer was slightly shocked and had to say, "Okay."

Issues to discuss: According to the case, do you think Zhang Lili will pass the interview? If not, what are the possible causes?

Case 2: When participating in the recruitment fair, Xiao Qiang, who has majored in international trade, entered the interview site of a well-known domestic enterprise. The competition for jobs was said to be fierce, with more than 300 resumes, only about 30 were qualified for interviews. When answering the interviewer's questions in groups of three, Xiao Qiang felt he had to be more active in order to stand out. So when answering questions, Xiao Qiang always grabbed the front of others to say more words. The interviewer saw this and asked him, "What if you have a problem with your colleague?" Xiao Qiang answered without thinking: "The work is the most important, and the contradiction between colleagues does not matter." A week later he was told that he did not have to take the re-examination.

Issues to discuss: Please analyze the reasons for the failure of Xiao Qiang's interview.

Chapter Two Business Conference Etiquette 会务礼仪

学习任务

1. 了解洽谈会中的礼仪要求。
2. 了解发布会中的礼仪要求。
3. 了解展销会中的礼仪要求。

Conference/meeting is a kind of social activity among two or more people, which relates to social contact, public relations, politics, interpersonal and intrapersonal communication and mass media.

It's commonly acknowledged that meeting is one type of social science as well as part of humanities and arts. In this chapter, there are three major conferences that will be introduced.

成功与失败，在于与会者及各方的诚意及能力。

I. Negotiation Conference 洽谈会

Contents:

1. Principles in business negotiation conference
2. Requirements in business negotiation conference
3. Procedures in business negotiation conference

Business negotiation conference is one of the most important business affairs.

洽谈，是指在商务交往中，存在着某种关系的有关各方，为了保持接触、建立联系、进行合作、达成交易、拟定协议、签署合同、要求索赔，或是为了处理争端、消除分歧，而坐在一起进行面对面的接洽与协商，以求达成某种程度上的妥协。因洽谈而进行的有关各方的会晤，便称为洽谈会。

To contact
To connect
To cooperate
To make a deal
To settle differences

1. Principles

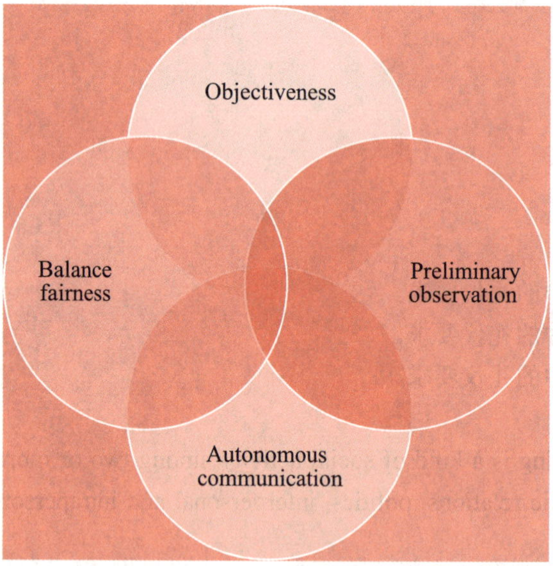

2. Requirements

礼敬对手
依法办事
平等协商

求同存异
互惠互利
人事分开

3. Procedures

3.1 Preparation

洽谈开始前的准备工作是必不可少的，是保证洽谈过程顺利进行的关键一步。

3.1.1 To evaluate the background information, preferences and taboos of the other party

Unfamiliarity→Misunderstanding→Insult→Failure

3.1.2 Choose a suitable location for the negotiation

A. Based on the guest's requirement

B. Based on the host's requirement

C. Rotation

D. Other choices

3.1.3 Seating arrangement

1) Wrap-round seats

- No platform, chairs, sofas or tables are randomly arranged, without precedence.
- Attendants can choose their seats freely.
- Similar to tea forum.

2) Free arrangement

- Similar to outdoor tea party/reading party.
- Seats and tables are optionally placed.
- The most comfortable and relaxed social environment.

3) Round-table arrangement

- One oval table is placed in the middle.
- Some round tables are arranged; attendants can choose their seats.

4) Platform

Chairman, presenter, and anchorman are arranged in the middle of the conference room.

3.2 During the negotiation

商务洽谈的过程不仅仅是语言上的交流，细节在其中决定着成败。想要立于不败之地，切忌将全部精力只放在条款或内容上，因为“千里之堤，毁于蚁穴”。(《韩非子·喻老》)

3.2.1 Proper attire

选择合适的服装出席一方面表达了对场合、双方的尊重，同时也能为你增添自信。

3.2.2 Keys to fair negotiation

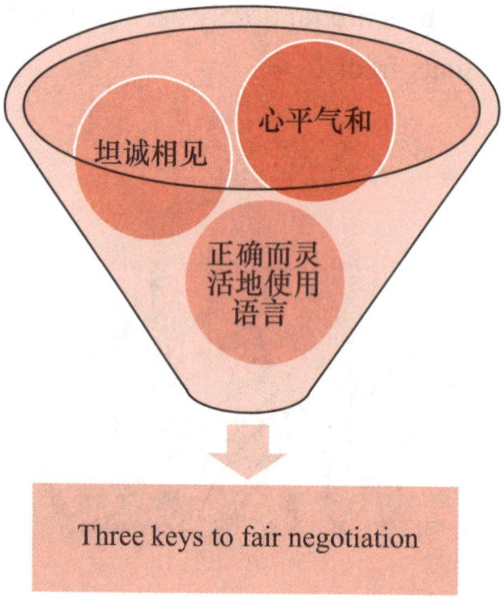

3.2.3 Taboos

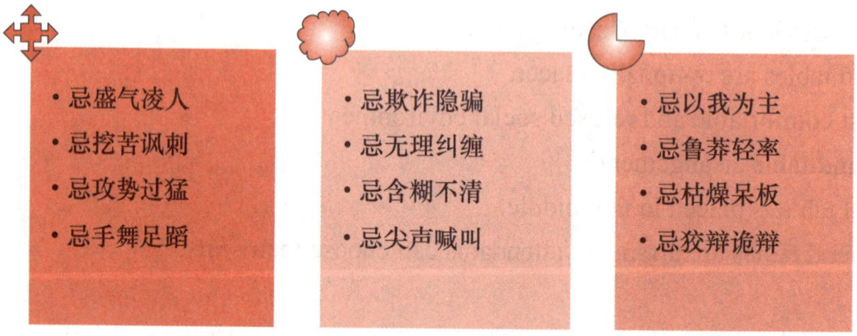

3.3 After business negotiation

Business negotiation should not be limited to the negotiation table. Keeping contact with the counter party is a key to a successful business relationship.

It is courtesy to send a timely follow-up e-mail after a business negotiation, and it is a good opportunity to summarize and clarify the agreement that both parties reached at the meeting, including the items discussed, action to be taken, and term and conditions that had been confirmed in a written form. Appreciation for the time, efforts and collaboration from the counter party should also be extended in the e-mail. Finally, the expectation for next meeting and the wish for the long-lasting business relationship should be expressed.

A Follow-up E-mail Template:

Subject: Meeting recap
Hi [Name],

It was a pleasure meeting with you today. Thank you for taking the time out of your busy schedule to discuss (topic) with us. I just wanted to follow up on our meeting with a few things.
Today we discussed (summary) and came up with these next steps (actionable items).
Please let me know if I missed anything.
Any questions at all, don't hesitate to reach out!
Looking forward to working together to meet your goals.
Best,
[Your name]

II. Press Conference 发布会

Contents:

1. Preparation for press conference
2. Things to be noticed

Press Conference refers to the conference which involves certain organizations or institutions, held to publish some major events or issues that may cause great effects. It can either improve the public image of the group or create some positive outcomes.

1. Preparation

1.1 Materials of related issues (paper or electronic versions)

为了应付突发情况的出现，完整、全面的资料是不可或缺的。注意：最好同时准备纸质资料和电子文件。

1.2 Hosts and presenters

会议的主持人需做到对流程及与会内容、人士的全面了解；发言人应言之有序，简明扼要，忌长篇大论，滔滔不绝。

1.3 Delivery of invitations

如非突发事件，应提前一周左右（最短不可少于 3 个工作日）给与会嘉宾发送邀请函，以便对方安排行程，同时方便主办方应对不可抗因素的出现（天气、嘉宾因故缺席等问题）。

1.4 Headlines of the conference: banner

发布会的布景板或者横幅上的内容需再三确认，提前备齐，以免错漏。

1.5 Preparation of other facilities

- Facilities should be checked before the conference to ensure no malfunctions.
- Site preparation and test should be pre-arranged. Guiding boards and conference greeters have to be set.
- Conference background plate should coincide with the theme.

2. Things Need to Be Noticed in the Scene

2.1 Host：appearance and language

主持人需注重仪容仪表：女士需化淡妆，建议着正装（具体请参照着装章节），男士发型忌夸张。措辞有礼而不奉承，不可喧宾夺主。

2.2 Post-conference：

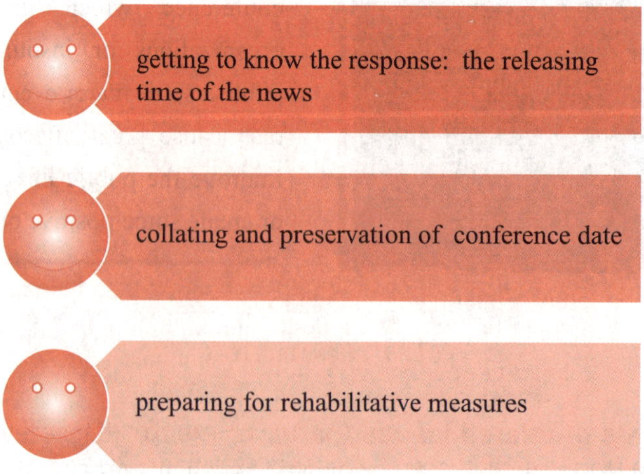

III. Commodities Fair/Exhibition 展销会

Contents:

1. Etiquette of spectators
2. Trade show booth etiquette

1. Etiquette of Spectators

以观众的质量评判展会的好坏已经成为惯性化的价值标准之一。

1.1 Primary concerns

Punctuality
Dignified dress
Moderate behavior
Concentration
Rules and orders

1.2 Different rules for different groups of participants

1.2.1 Professional:

确定参观路线
确定拟了解的信息
设计信息收集表
确定参观时间
介绍自己，派发并收集名片
避开过于拥挤的展位，寻找机会再访
记录信息
与参展商洽谈

1.2.2 Ordinary:

根据展览时间的具体日程，合理安排工作，按时参加展览活动
未经允许，不应随意触摸和拿走展品
对展位接待人员讲解及服务应礼貌回应
不哄抢展品

2. Trade Show Booth Etiquette

Attending trade show is an important way for companies to attain leads. Trade show etiquette gives potential business partners and visitors a good first impression, attracts more visitors, gains leads, thus leaves up the expectation of attending exhibition. The staff in booth is a key element and the reason why visitors leave or stay.

2.1 Staff in the trade show booth should

- follow the staff dress code,
- welcome every visitor by standing up and smiling ,
- be familiar with the company and the products or services, and introduce them enthusiastically and friendly,
- and express thanks to the visitors for their attention and time.

2.2 Staff in the trade show booth should avoid

- drinking and eating in the booth, and providing any food to other staff,
- swiping cellphones,
- chatting with staff of other booths but ignoring the visitors,
- and being late for the show or disappearing from the booth before the end of the show.

Exercise 章节练习

1. Scene simulation practice

Directions: Suppose you participate in a business conference, practice the skills of self-introduction and introduction of your boss/host and customers.

2. Case study

Case 1

Directions: Discuss in groups and make a reception plan:

In one ASEAN Expo, your group will be responsible for receiving a team of 15 business representatives from the Philippines. Your guests carried much luggage and followed you to the parking lot of the airport, which took them a long time to get there. However, you finally found out that there was an express elevator. Afterwards, you could not locate your car and driver. Moreover, when they finally got into the car, their luggage could not fit in the car that was assigned for them. At that moment, their complaints were heard everywhere in spite of your repeated apology.

Issues to discuss: 1) What are the complaints? How to deal with them?

2) If you are the liaison man, what will you do? What is your reception plan?

Case 2

Directions: Read the news report on the PR crisis that BMW Mini faced because of their staff's misbehavior in their booth at auto show and discuss:

1) What were the problems with the booth staff in BMW mini booth?

2) Some observers believed that rather than discrimination against Chinese people, the incident demonstrated the xenophilia that still exists in Chinese society. To what extent do you agree with the statement?

yahoo!finance Search for news, symbols or companies

In this article:

TSLA +1.02% WB -3.81%

The BMW Mini booth at Shanghai's auto show—the first since China's reopening in December—had a nice freebie for attendees: a small tub of ice cream from a local brand.

More from Fortune: 5 side hustles where you may earn over $20,000 per year—all while working from home Looking to make extra cash? This CD has a 5.15% APY right now Buying a house? Here's how much to save This is how much money you need to earn annually to comfortably buy a $600,000 home

But the free snack ended up causing a headache for the German carmaker after a video from the show was posted on Bilibili, a YouTube-like platform in China. The recording shows the staff running the booth telling one local visitor that all the ice cream had been given away. When a foreign attendee arrived, staff suddenly had ice cream on hand.

The incident, which state-run media outlet *Global Times* reported happening on Wednesday evening, went viral on Chinese social media, with one hashtag "BMW Mini booth accused of discrimination" attracting almost 200 million views on China's Twitter-like Weibo platform, according to the *Financial Times*.

BMW Mini apologized on Thursday, saying that "sloppy internal management" and "our staff's failure of duty" caused "unpleasantness," in a post to the company's Weibo account, according to the *Financial Times*. The company later said that Mini "condemns racism and intolerance in any form."

A company spokesperson told *Fortune* that the booth had halted the ice cream giveaway owing to low stock, and the foreign attendee who received one of the last remaining tubs was an acquaintance of one of the hostesses. The company again apologized.

The German carmaker's shares fell 3.6% on Thursday. By 11:30 a.m. Berlin time on Friday, shares were largely flat.

Chapter Three

Etiquette in a Business Ceremony

行业仪式礼仪

学习任务

1. 了解签约仪式中的礼仪要求。
2. 了解剪彩仪式中的礼仪要求。
3. 了解开业典礼中的礼仪要求。

I. Signing Ceremony 签约

Contents:

1. The process of a signing ceremony
2. The etiquette in a signing ceremony

Warm-up:

Scan the QR code to watch the following video and try to find out the mistakes in the signing ceremony.

1. The Process of a Signing Ceremony

A signing ceremony is a formal occasion at which a significant document is formally signed, and often involves different departments, organizations, companies or countries. Short but formal, a signing ceremony requires a good preparation to ensure that it goes smoothly.

1.1 The preparation of a signing ceremony

Before the signing ceremony, the host needs to get the following things ready.

1.1.1 The guests present

The host should arrange its members present according to the identities and the number of the guests present, especially for the signers of honor. And the host should also have the accommodation arranged for the guests and choose the lodging near the site of the signing ceremony.

> 在确定了双方出席人员以后，应向客方通报双方人员的名单。

Specialists such as notaries and lawyers can also be invited if it is necessary.

1.1.2 The site of the signing ceremony

- 签约地点一般安排在宾馆、酒店、会客厅、会议室等场地。
- 在签约厅设置长桌作为签字桌，覆盖台布，放置签约人就座的椅子，签约厅内提供足够的椅子供随行人员就座。
- 桌上放置合同。如果是国家间的签约仪式，则应该准备好各方的国旗置于桌上。
- 在确定了签约地点以后，应向客方通报。

If it is a bilateral signing ceremony, you may have the site layout in the following two ways.

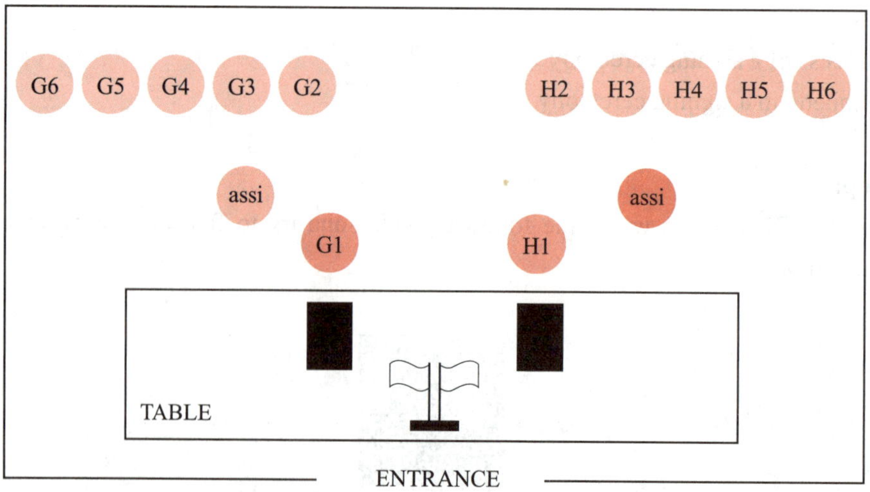

(G: Guest; H: Host; assi: assistant)

方式一：主左客右。
双方随行人员站立于签约人身后。
签约助理分别站立于两位签约人外侧斜后方。

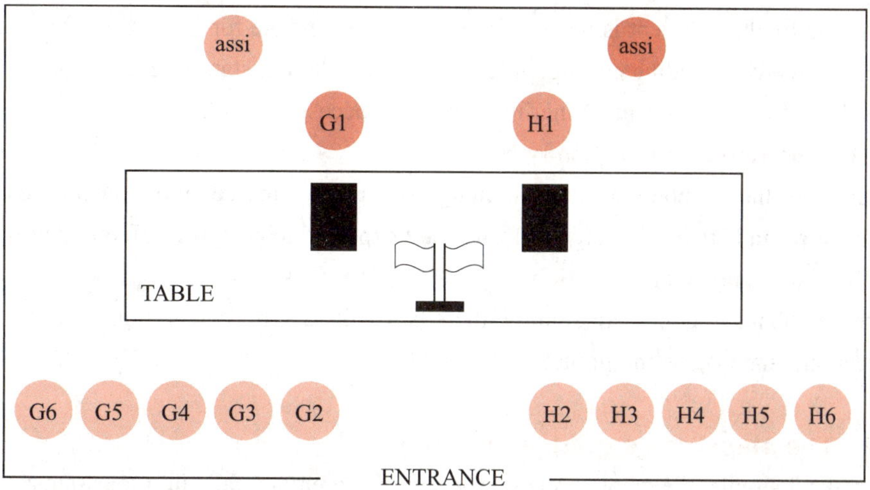

方式二：主左客右
双方随行人员就座于签约人对面。
签约助理分别站立于两位签约人斜后方。

If it is a multilateral signing ceremony, you may have the site set up in this way.

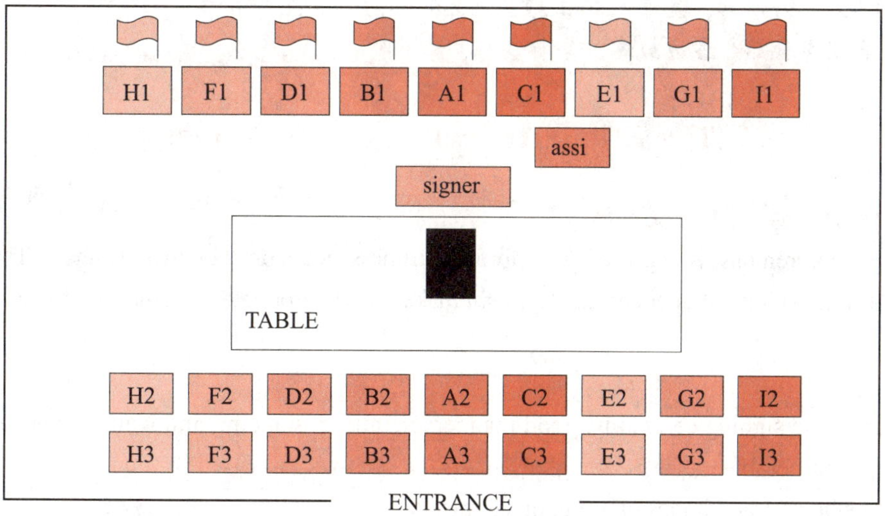

方式：设置一个签约人座位。
各方轮流到签约桌前签字。

各方签约人在签约桌后方就座，座位后方分别放置对应的国旗。
各方随行人员分别于本国签约人的对面就座。

1.1.3 The document

After the final agreement is reached, the host is responsible for getting the final edition of the document ready, including editing, proofreading, translating, stamping and binding.

Besides the document, some other items are also necessary, such as pens.

1.1.4 The staff of the ceremony

Apart from the members of the host and guests, the signing ceremony also needs an MC, some ritual girls and other backstage staff, who are expected to perform different duties.

1.1.5 The items for celebration

After the phase of document signing, there is usually a short celebration in which camera, video recorder, champagne and goblets are needed.

1.2 The steps of a signing ceremony

To make it simple, the whole process of a signing ceremony falls into four steps:

seating → signing → exchanging → celebrating

1. 签约各方进场。签约人在签约桌前就座，其余人员在签约人身后按照级别从高到低、由里往外站立，或者按照座位安排就座。
2. 仪式开始前，往往会安排高层或领导发表致辞。
3. 签字仪式开始，各方签约人在合约上签字。助理负责递送签字笔、指出具体签字的位置。一方签好以后助理辅助签约人与对方交换合同，签约人再次签字。
4. 各方签好以后，签字人起立郑重地交换合同，并握手留影。
5. 合同交换后，各方鼓掌并举杯庆祝。

2. The Etiquette in a Signing Ceremony

2.1 Attire and grooming

Signing ceremony is regarded as a formal business occasion though it is short. Therefore, formal business suit is a proper choice. And light make-up is appropriate for female in this occasion.

2.2 Proper behaviors

During the signing ceremony, good manners in sitting, standing and walking and smile on the face are preferable.

Keep the mobile phones on mute or vibrate.

Be attentive. Refrain from staring at the mobile phone, chatting or reading a book etc. Get involved in the whole process of the ceremony.

II. Ribbon-Cutting Ceremony 剪彩

Contents:

1. The process of a ribbon-cutting ceremony
2. The etiquette in a ribbon-cutting ceremony

Warm-up:

Please decide which ones of the following are proper behaviors in a ribbon-cutting ceremony.

1. If one of the guests for a ribbon-cutting ceremony fails to be present because of emergencies, look for a makeweight at once to fill out the numbers.

2. The host should book the hotel for the guests.

3. A ribbon-cutting ceremony is not a formal business occasion, so we can choose the dresses for social occasions.

4. Each guest has his own place when cutting the ribbon. According to the international rules, the right side is of priority, so the rightmost place should be reserved for the guest of honor.

5. In order to extend the sincere welcome to the guest, the host has to arrange a grand celebration.

6. Both the outdoor site and the indoor site are OK for a ribbon-cutting ceremony.

7. If it is an outdoor ceremony, it is acceptable to wear sunglasses in the sunlight.

8. When foreign guests are invited to the ribbon-cutting ceremony, their national flag(s) should be on the preparation list.

1. The Process of a Ribbon-cutting Ceremony

A ribbon-cutting ceremony is a public ceremony to celebrate the opening to the general public of a new project, including the opening or anniversary of a company or a shop, foundation stone laying ceremony, the completion of a public building, the operation of transportation or infrastructure, etc. The ribbon cutting is merely metaphorical.

关于剪彩的由来，有两种说法：

一种说法是，古代的欧洲造船业比较发达，新船下水会吸引很多人参观。为防止意外发生，通常在离船较远处拉起一根绳。到典礼准备就绪后，就会剪断绳索让人们靠近参观。

另一种说法是，美国乡村的一家商店准备开业，老板为了防止人们争相抢购优惠商品，便在门框上拉起一条布条，却不料这样更激发了人们的好奇心。就在这时，老板的小女儿牵着的小狗不小心将布条碰落，人们误以为是为开张庆典设计的小花招，于是一拥而入，老板看着生意出奇地红火，马上转怒为喜。

剪彩用的绳索、布条后来都改为了彩带，剪彩者也由主持人、小狗变为儿童、少女，最后演变为社会名流、高层领导等。

1.1 The preparation of a ribbon-cutting ceremony

The preparation of a ribbon-cutting ceremony includes:

1.1.1 The celebrity guest and the ceremony staff

The guests invited to the ribbon-cutting ceremony are usually of prominent social status with distinguished contributions and good reputations in certain fields. With deliberation, the host should decide whom to be invited to the ceremony and send out the invitation as soon as possible, because it looks unprofessional to have makeweights for the ceremony. For some occasions, only one guest is invited, while for others, several guests are invited.

The ceremony staff refers to the assistants helping to finish the ribbon-cutting ceremony, such as the serving assistants and the ritual girls who are in charge of holding the ribbon, passing the scissors and guiding the way. Training of the staff is necessary or hiring the professional ceremony staff is also a good choice.

1.1.2 The site of the ribbon-cutting ceremony

The ribbon-cutting ceremony is usually held at the site of the project to be celebrated. The spacious place is preferable, such as square, hall etc.

Before the ceremony, the host should have the site layout and the ceremonial stuffs ready. Banners, ribbon, scissors, background music, as well as audio equipment are necessities and ceremony crackers, chairs and national flags are optional.

1.2 The steps of a ribbon-cutting ceremony

To make it simple, the whole process of a ribbon-cutting ceremony falls into three steps:

addressing → ribbon cutting → celebrating

1. 剪彩嘉宾进场。礼仪小姐将剪彩嘉宾带至嘉宾席，按照座次顺序落座。

2. 主持人宣布仪式开始，并邀请上级领导、主办方代表、合作方代表以及剪彩嘉宾代表等上台致辞。

3. 剪彩仪式开始。由礼仪小姐将剪彩嘉宾引领至彩带后面安排好的位置（按照国际惯例：中间高于两侧，右侧高于左侧），剪彩嘉宾同时剪断彩带。

4. 剪彩完成。鸣放花炮，全场鼓掌。其后进行后续庆典，如祝酒、就餐、文艺表演、签名题字、参观等。

2. Etiquette in a Ribbon-cutting Ceremony

2.1 Attire and grooming

Like the signing ceremony, a ribbon-cutting ceremony is also short but formal. Therefore, formal business dress is still the best choice. However, one social style is also acceptable, especially for ladies, who will be graceful in mandarin gowns or morning social dresses.

A light make-up is suggested. Sunglasses and hats are not appropriate.

2.2 Proper behaviors

Proper manners in sitting, standing and walking are preferable. The ceremony guests are expected to take their own place behind the ribbon orderly, with a smile on their faces and casual mannerisms.

Keep the mobile phones on mute or vibrate.

Just like what is required in the signing ceremony, all the members present should be attentive and focusing.

III. Opening Ceremony 开业

Contents:

1. The features and functions of an opening ceremony
2. The etiquette in an opening ceremony

The opening ceremony refers to the inauguration ceremony of a company or a building, and it also symbolizes kind of completion, commemoration, or celebration.

开业仪式是按照一定的程序隆重举行的专门的仪式。

1. Features and Functions of an Opening Ceremony

1.1 Features

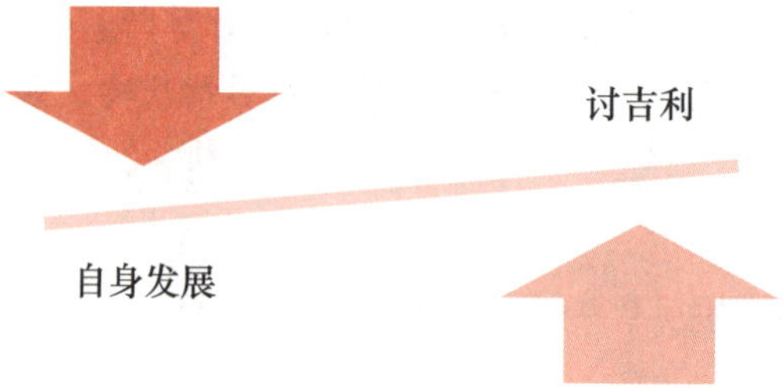

1.2 Functions

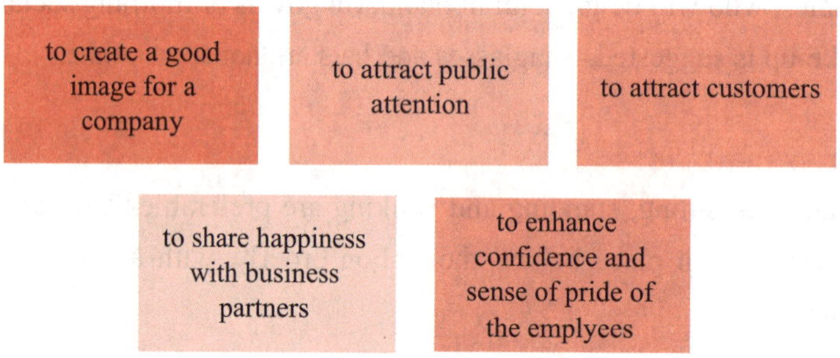

2. Etiquette in an Opening Ceremony

一般是指在开业仪式筹备与活动的具体过程中应当遵从的礼仪惯例。

Two items are involved: preparation and procedure

2.1 Preparation

Principles: **enthusiasm, parsimony, meticulousness**

2.2 Procedure

In this part, three basic and commonly performed ceremonies will be discussed.

2.2.1 The opening ceremony

The opening ceremony of a company or an organization is the most common one in the field of business.

通常它是指公司、企业、宾馆、商店、银行正式启用之前，或各类商品的展示会、博览会、订货会正式开始之前，所正式举行的相关仪式。

☐ After that, the company/organization will be in formal business, exhibition/exposition/order-placing conference will officially entertain customers and spectators.

☐ Generally speaking, capacious and comfortable activity space will be needed. Therefore, plaza/hall/lobby of the exhibition hall can be used as the location of the opening ceremony.

Procedure:

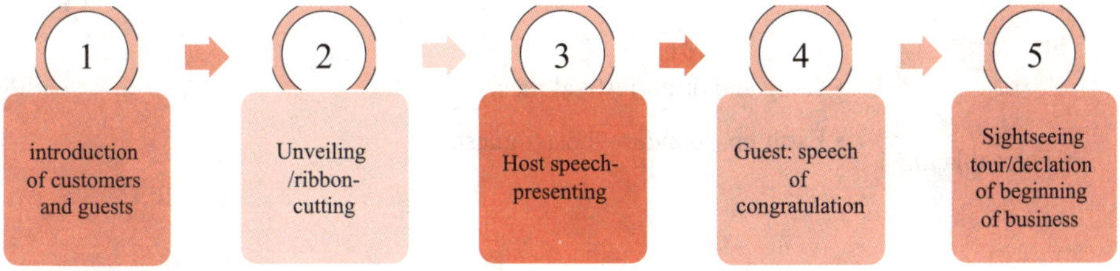

2.2.2 The foundation stone laying ceremony

Before certain significant constructions are built, such as mansions, stadiums, pavilions, terraces, open halls, parks or gardens, and monuments, a kind of official activity is held in order to celebrate.

The foundation stone should be placed on the RIGHT side of the main entrance/front gate.

In China, there are some rules of this stone.

用以奠基的奠基石应为一块完整无损、外观精美的长方形石料，文字应当竖写。

右上款，应刻有建筑物的正式名称；正中央应刻有“奠基”两个大字。

左下款，应刻有奠基单位的全称以及举行奠基仪式的具体年月日。

字体，以楷体字刻写，最好是白底金字或黑字。

在奠基石的下方或一侧，还应安放一只密闭完好的铁盒，内装有与该建筑物的各项资料以及奠基人的姓名。届时，它将同奠基石一道被奠基人等培土掩埋于地下，以志纪念。

In the ceremony, the model, design paper/design sketch, even construction machinery should be in placed and stand by.

Procedure:

第一项，仪式正式开始。介绍来宾，全体起立。

第二项，奏国歌。

第三项，主人对该建筑物的功能以及规划设计进行简介。

第四项，来宾致辞道喜。

第五项，正式进行奠基。此时，应锣鼓喧天，或演奏喜庆乐曲。首先由奠基人双手持握系有红绸的新锨为奠基石培土。随后，再由主人与其他嘉宾依次为之培土，直至将其埋没为止。

2.2.3 The completion ceremony

The completion ceremony refers to the ceremony that is held for a building/facility, in order to celebrate its completion/installation. Besides, the ceremony is also held when a kind of product, which contains specific or significant meaning, is successfully completed.

Location: construction/installation site

Procedure:

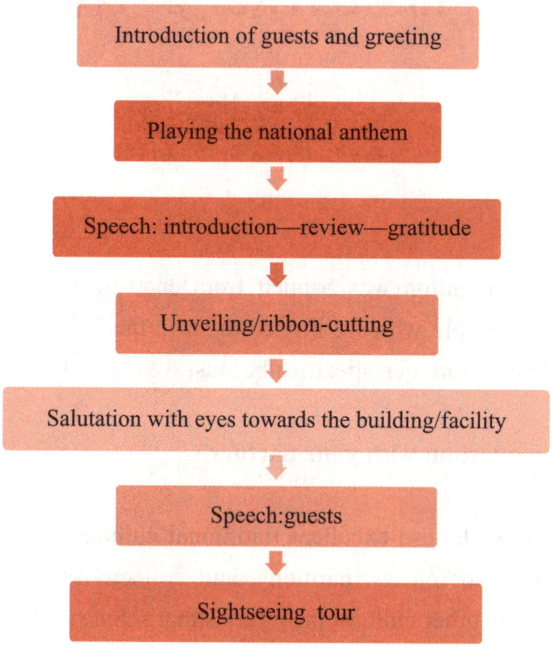

Exercise 章节练习

Directions:

The students in the class are going to work in three teams, each of which is assigned to plan a signing ceremony or a ribbon-cutting ceremony or an opening ceremony.

All teams are required to put their plans into words, practice and perform. When one team finishes its performance, other teams give comments.

Key to Exercise 参考答案

Module One

Warm-up:

1. Q&A

Key for reference:

C is Correct. Lewis Hamilton was banned from entering the Royal Box as he wasn't wearing the correct attire. People who are invited to sit in the Royal Box on Centre Court are required to wear formal attire and men specifically must wear a jacket, tie and shoes.

2. Discuss the following question with your partner.

Key for reference:

We can carry forward Chinese excellent traditional culture by promoting its values and principles, such as respect for elders, harmony, and collectivism. We can do this through education, art, literature, and other cultural institutions that showcase the beauty and richness of Chinese heritage. For example, new media should be used to spread Chinese excellent traditional etiquette education. Family, school and society should pay attention to traditional etiquette education.

Strengthening cultural self-confidence involves embracing our unique cultural identity and promoting it globally. This means not only celebrating our achievements but also acknowledging our shortcomings and working to overcome them. It also means being open to learning from other cultures and incorporating their best practices into our own traditions. By doing so, we can build a more diverse and inclusive society that values and respects different cultures and perspectives. Only by truly understanding the essence and excellence of our etiquette can we have a sense of respect and pride for our excellent culture; only with the courage to absorb and transform foreign culture can we have a sense of respect and self-confidence for the development and prosperity of the Chinese national culture and actively strive to practice it.

Exercise

Discussion 1:

Try to use the basic knowledge of etiquette to talk about your feelings about Chinese historical story of "负荆请罪" (voluntarily offer to be punished with the rod).

Key for reference:

1. Tolerance can turn an enemy into a friend. Lin Xiangru tolerated Lian Po's jealousy and

won Lian Po's respect with his noble virtue. It was Lin Xiangru's tolerance that made Lian Po feel ashamed of himself, apologizing for his sins, and thus achieving the perfect ending of the peace between the generals.

2. The overall situation and national interests should always be put first. Lin Xiangru's broad-mindedness of putting national interests first made Lian Po feel ashamed. Lian Po apologized and became friends with Lin Xiangru.

Discussion 2:

Key for reference:

It means that etiquette should conform to the times and should not be outdated. In modern society, economic development is an important topic. Seizing the opportunity to seek economic development needs to seize the pulse of the times and grasp the needs and trends of the market, and constantly innovate and improve their products and services. This requires us to constantly learn and improve our ability, understand the changes and trends of the market, and adjust our business strategy in time to meet the needs of the market. At the same time, we also need to pay attention to the construction of corporate culture, establishing a good corporate image and brand image, and improve customer satisfaction and loyalty.

Module Two

Chapter One Dress Etiquette

Exercise

1. Discussion

1) Please talk about your understanding of the saying "Apparel makes the man".

Key for reference:

"People rely on clothing, while horses rely on saddles". This is an old Chinese saying, which means that wearing appropriate clothes will make people appear energetic. This saying emphasizes the importance of appearance, especially when meeting for the first time, appearance is often the key to creating a good first impression. Therefore, we should pay attention to our appearance, not only to make ourselves feel beautiful, but also to show respect for others.

2) Yeda is a new employee and today is her first day in an insurance company. Are these dresses appropriate? And why?

Key for reference:

The dress of professionals should follow the TPO principle, which refers to time, place and occasion.

a. Time principle. Daytime is often the working time. Therefore, the dress should naturally be chosen according to the nature of your work. No matter what kind of work, it should be generous and solemn.

b. Place principle. Dress should be in accordance with the space and environment you will enter and leave. For example, if you want to go to the site to inspect the construction progress, you'd better choose a capable suit.

c. Occasion principle. Clothing should conform to the specifications and atmosphere of the event. A pair of casual shoes cannot go with a formal and serious negotiation meeting, otherwise it will be considered that you don't pay attention to the interests of the company, and thus you will be disgusted.

3) Scan the QR code to watch the video and discuss the following questions.

Key for reference:

Q1: When matching make-up and costumes, the two girls fully considered the promising occasions and places. For example, Gloria's work clothes and dating clothes are very different, and some changes have been made in make-up.

Q2: Make-up and costume collocation should complement each other. Style attributes of different shades of make-up. The colors of clothes correspond to different styles. Similarly, the colors of make-up also have different and specific feelings. Clothing is closely related to make-up modeling. Clothing products include various accessories, such as earrings, necklaces, bracelets, rings, etc., while make-up modeling refers to creating your own image through make-up and hairstyle. Clothing products can play the role of ornament and foil, and can enhance the fashion sense and personality charm of the overall shape. For example, choosing suitable earrings and necklaces can make the facial contour more prominent, and choosing bracelets and rings can increase the charm of hands. Clothing products can also echo with make-up modeling to create a style or theme together. For example, with exquisite make-up and gorgeous jewelry, you can show a noble and elegant image; simple and clean make-up and simple accessories can create a fresh and natural feeling.

4) Discuss the incident.

Key for reference:

Dior's arrogant behavior not only reflects their lack of respect for Chinese culture and the Chinese market, but also prompts us to reflect. Without this incident, many Chinese people may not have known that horse face skirts are our traditional clothing. Protecting and inheriting national culture is urgent, and what we need to do is to make everyone understand, love, and spontaneously inherit and promote *Hanfu* culture, so that *Hanfu* can truly integrate into our daily lives. Xu Jiao's appearance on the red carpet of the Golden Rooster Award in the horse face skirt is a good example, making the horse face skirt once again amazing and well-known. Nowadays, more and more people are beginning to understand and like *Hanfu*, and joining the ranks of guarding traditional culture, which is a manifestation of cultural confidence. However, many people's love for *Hanfu* only stays in appreciation but not wearing. This indicates that the promotion of *Hanfu* still faces some problems. For example, some people think that it makes one look beautiful but inconvenient to move with *Hanfu* on; some people may think it is weird to wear *Hanfu* because not so many people wear it, and some feels that the price of *Hanfu* is a bit high.

2. Case study:

Referring to the principle of TPO and answer the question: Why are proper dresses so important?

Key for reference:

TPO principle is an internationally recognized dressing principle. TPO is the abbreviation of three English words: time, place and occasion. It means that when people choose clothes and consider their specific styles, they should first give consideration to time, place and purpose, and strive to make their own clothes and their specific styles coordinate with the time, place and purpose of clothes, so as to achieve a harmonious match. In today's workplace in China, more and more young people are beginning to pay attention to their mental outlook, hoping to boost their spirits through handsome clothes in the stressful workplace. Neat and decent clothes are very important for a person in the workplace. Don't think that you can be sloppy or overly casual without facing the position of external communication. That will "help yourself" and the enterprise. Many times, we will give people the impression of "not serious" and "unprofessional" because of the image of the other party's clothes, thus showing our worries and doubts about this enterprise and the person in charge of the other party, which may directly affect the development of the business.

Mr. Mo Yan's Swallow-tailed Coat

Why did Mo Yan choose a swallow-tailed coat for Nobel Prize Award ceremony instead of the dresses recommended by Chinese netizens?

Key for reference:

The reason why Mo Yan chose a swallow-tailed coat is that Nobel Prize award ceremony is a very formal international occasion which was held in the evening. And all the Nobel Prize winners were dressed in white tie, which is considered the international dress code for the most formal occasion, no matter which nation they came from. So, it is not proper for Mo Yan to wear the Chinese traditional dresses.

3. After-class activity (critical thinking)

Key for reference:

Cultural confidence is more of a basic, profound and enduring confidence. Culture is the crystal of a national character and soul, which relates to a nation's survival and revitalization.

Cultural confidence are the new key words for China's cultural development that generate strategic importance to Chinese and global development, which is based on the cultural needs and creations of the people that stand for inheriting an excellent traditional culture and developing innovation to step onto the world stage.

Clothing is closely related to human, and since ancient times, clothing has played an extremely important role in Chinese culture. Clothing, which not only protects people from cold but also carries the meaning of "etiquette", ranks first among the basic needs of human life such as "clothing, food, housing, and transportation". As an important component of traditional Chinese culture, traditional costume creates a strong sense of identity among people, and its revival is helping to establish and enhance our confidence in culture.

Chapter Two　Grooming

Exercise

1. Classify the following pictures into "Dos" and "Don'ts" on business occasions.

Key for reference:

Dos: A, F, H

Don'ts: B, C, D, E, G, I

2. Tutorial

Basic steps of make-up:

1) Clean your face (get ready for a make-up).

2) Skincare:

  a. toner: moisturize your skin;

  b. lotion, serum, eye cream and cream

3) Premier: enrich your skin color;

4) Foundation: adjust the skin color, cover some defect and smoothen skin;

5) Concealer: cover up small flaws on your skin;

6) Setting powder: loose powder and pressed powder are both fine, and they both show long-lasting effect.

7) Eye shadow/eye liner: deepen and highlight the eyes;

8) Mascara

9) Eyebrow pencil: draw your favorite eyebrow shape;

10) Blusher and lipstick.

Make-up will generally be adjusted and changed with the occasion. For example, on some important social occasions such as banquets, it is recommended to appropriately enhance the color of your eye shadow or lipstick based on the color of clothing. On daily social occasions, people prefer a nude look. Earth tone is generally recommended for eye shadow in the workplace and the color of lipstick can be brick red and rose pink.

3. Scan the QR code to watch the video clip and try to notice what the wrong doings are in attire and grooming.

Key for reference:

Wrong doing 1: Jack is wearing a pair of white socks.

Wrong doing 2: Anita and Jack don't take off their hats.

Wrong doing 3: Both Anita and Jack put their bags on the chair behind them.

Other wrong doings: Anita doesn't mute her phone and answers the phone call in front of her business partner.

Module Three

Chapter One Etiquette in Greeting

I. Greeting

Warm-up:

How do they greet each other in the following pictures? Do you know some other ways of greeting?

Key for reference:

The two people in the picture are shaking hands. I also know the other ways including hugging, bowing, bisou and so on.

II. Exchanging Business Cards

Warm-up:

Case: In the business communication, people exchange cards at the first meeting, which helps to establish business contact and shows respect and self-cultivation to each other.

Key for reference:

The suggested way to pass a business card can be as follows:

When submitting a business card, you should hold the left and right ends of the business card with your index finger and thumb, stare at each other with your eyes open, smile, and bow down. Patch pocket is not the place to keep the business card and it is impolite to take a business card directly from a patch pocket of the upper suit.

When you accept a business card, you should take a look at it carefully and repeat the name and position on the business card in a low voice.

After receiving the business card, you should also express your gratitude to the other party, and then seriously put the business card in the business card holder or in your coat pocket. Don't throw it on the table or play with it in your hand.

III. Etiquette in Gifting

Warm-up:

1. What is the etiquette in receiving gifts?

Key for reference:

Stand up immediately and face each other when one announces a gift. Don't reach out before the announcer takes out of the gift. Receive the gift with both hands, smile and keep eye contact. Then hold the gift with left hand (large gift could be put down), and shake hands with right hand to thank the gift-giver.

2. What kind of gifts do you think are not acceptable? How to refuse them?

Key for reference:

(Open discussion) Possible answers: Money is not acceptable as a gift. Say no directly, explaining it is not allowed by the law of China.

Exercise

1. Discussion

Key for reference:

Peony is China's national flower and is an important element in Chinese culture, which is favored by all the Chinese. And the beauty and elegance of Peony is known and loved by the people all over the world. Chinese Go and Chess have a very long history in China, which represent the essence of traditional Chinese culture: friendliness and cooperation. Therefore, the Chinese government chose the two gifts to show Chinese culture and the friendship between China and France.

Chapter Two　Etiquette in Walking and Cars

I. Etiquette in Walking

Warm-up:

1. Have you ever noticed people's daily walking? Could you describe some walking details of different people and different occasions?

Key for reference:

It is an open-ended question and the following answer can be used as a reference.

Yes, I have noticed that the walking of different people is different. For soldiers, they walk with their chins up and chests out; for nurses, they always walk very fast; for teachers, they walk lightly; for men, they walk with vigorous strides. And people also walk differently in different occasions. In daily walking, people always walk casually; but in formal occasion, people usually pay much attention to their walking.

2. On business occasions, some etiquette in walking should be paid attention to. Could you use some examples to illustrate what you have known about the etiquette in walking?

Key for reference:

Open-ended question. For this question, students should be encouraged to say what they have known about walking etiquette, no matter whether the answer is right or wrong. The following answer can be used as a reference.

For example, the younger always walk behind the elder; the leader always walks in front; eating while waking is inappropriate; lady first, etc.

II. Etiquette in Cars

Warm-up:

How to arrange the car seats in a business trip?

Picture 1: B-Mr. Smith, D-Mrs. Smith

Picture 2: E-Mr. Smith, D-Mrs. Smith

Exercise

2. Practice

Practice in groups to simulate sitting and getting on and off the car. The following are several situations, which can be practiced and arranged by students respectively.

1) Three for the foreign side (marketing manager, assistant marketing manager, secretary), two for our side (interpreter, driver), they take one car driven by the owner.

2) Five for the foreign side (deputy general manager, marketing manager, assistant marketing manager, secretary A and secretary B), two for our side (interpreter and driver), they take one car driven by the full-time driver.

Key for reference:

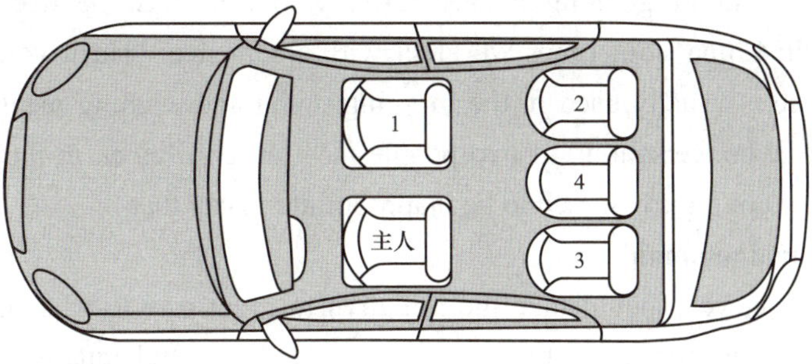

1-marketing manager　　2-assistant marketing manager

3-secretary　　4-interpreter

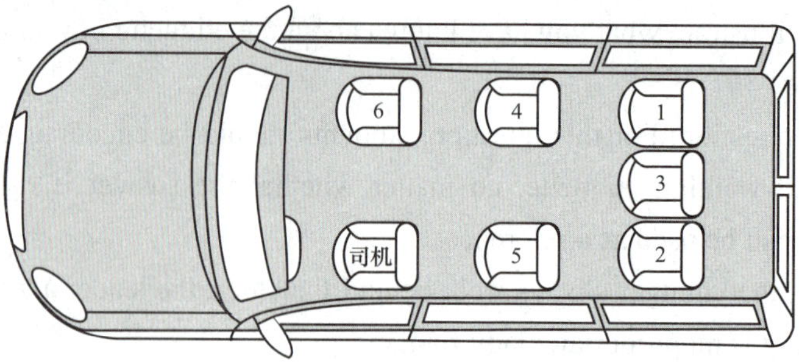

1-deputy general manager
2-marketing manager
3-assistant marketing manager
4-secretary A
5-secretary B
6-interpreter

Chapter Three Etiquette in Conversation

Exercise

1. Questions and discussion:

What should we pay attention to if we meet an acquaintance, or a business partner?

Key for reference:

Answers can be varied or based on the content of this chapter.

(Meeting with an acquaintance)

For example, in China, one of your colleagues, Xiao Wang wears a new suit. You can praise him: "Xiao Wang, you look beautiful in this suit!" If you meet an older friend or colleague, then you can say, "You look younger and energetic!" These compliment greetings are commonly seen. Because we believe that people need others' affirmation and recognition, and like such sincere and appropriate compliment, we can create a harmonious communication atmosphere through complimentary greetings.

If you meet a friend at the door or on the road in the morning, you can say, "Good morning! Going to work?" If you meet a friend in the canteen, you can say, "How are you today?" etc. This kind of greeting comes casually, but it must be decent and not used indiscriminately. In China, sometimes we greet with a sentence: "Have you eaten?" (你吃了吗?) This sentence is usually used in the morning, noon and evening meal time by Chinese people in their daily conversations. If two people meet at ten o'clock in the morning or three o'clock in the afternoon, it is believed to be inappropriate to say that.

(Meeting with a businessman)

(1) In the office, you should take the initiative to greet people who pass your desk, no matter whether they are colleagues or bosses, they should be treated equally.

(2) When the elevator meets the boss, you should take the initiative to greet him/her generously. It is not advisable to dodge or pretend not to see him/her. If a colleague greets you or meets your eyes, you should nod, smile and even respond at the right time. When the boss

talks to you, you should politely answer “Yes, Mr./Ms. XXX” or “Yes, Boss”.

(3) When you leave the office, you should remember to report to the supervisor and ask if there are any orders before you leave.

(4) Colleagues who are familiar with each other can greet each other in a way that they feel comfortable. They also can call each other by their first names if they get permission from each other, but they should not call each other by their nicknames in the workplace. Because these names contain jokes, it will make people feel disrespectful.

(5) When someone calls you, you should respond immediately. Even if you are answering the phone, you should put it down for a while and tell him that you are answering the phone and will come later.

2. Scan the QR codes to watch two video clips, and discuss the differences and importance of conducting conversations with different people.

Key for reference:

Greeting is a courtesy behavior when acquaintances meet on the road. But the way of greeting varies from country to country. In China, Chinese people like to ask “Have you eaten?” Or “Where are you going?” It is similar to “Hello!” If you answer “I haven’t eaten yet”, something is wrong. If you greet foreigners with it, it is often understood as “inviting me to dinner” and “having nothing to talk about”, which leads to misunderstanding. In Britain and America, when acquaintances or friends greet each other, they often say, “Hello, how are you?” Or talk about the weather: “Lovely weather, isn’t it? “Chinese people also like to ask each other’s name, place of origin, age, etc. However, in most cases, British and American people, regardless of gender, age and status, usually call each other by their first names even when they meet for the first time. The more common greeting is “How do you do?” “Nice to meet you” and so on. Its more commonly used farewell words are wishing each other an early recovery when visiting someone in the hospital. In China, certain topic is common to hear in daily conversation among acquaintances (such as age, marital status, how much money you earn, etc.), but it will cause the foreigners’ displeasure if you talk about these with them. Because in their culture, these topics has greatly violated the “privacy” of others.

The importance of conversation in interpersonal communication is irreplaceable. Conversation is a comprehensive reflection of people’s knowledge, experience, intelligence, education and adaptability.

Characteristics of conducting a conversation:

1) Be real and natural. 2) Get to know each other. 3) Mutual tolerance. 4) Information transmission. 5) The content is various.

- Pay attention to the voice of the conversation, greet and chat with people in the corridor, and don’t speak loudly, so as not to affect others.
- Pay attention to the conversation. When you speak, you can’t ignore the role of your

eyes. You should use your eyes to help expression, and you can also understand other people's emotions and feelings through their eyes. When speaking, the speaker should look at the other person's eyes and show sincerity and concentration, which is a respect for others. The range of gaze varies from occasion to occasion.

- Pay attention to the manners and content of conversation.

When talking, you can use appropriate gestures to strengthen your tone and help express yourself. Don't make unnecessary movements, which will affect the listener's attention. We should pay attention to the choice of content based on the occasion and the people that we talk to.

Chapter Five　Dining Etiquette

I. Formal Banquet

Warm-up

1. B　　2. D　　3. B　　4. D

Exercise

Discussion:

1. Scan the QR code to watch the video, and try to find out the rude behaviors in dining.

Key for reference:

Rude behaviors:

1) Katherine and Irene are late for the luncheon party.
2) Irene takes the seat before the hosts do so.
3) Katherine starts her meal before the hosts do so.
4) Irene talks to others with the food in her mouth.
5) Irene tries to discuss a private problem with Cloris.
6) Katherine asks about Rita's wages.
7) Katherine answers a private phone call in front of the hosts.
8) They don't hold the wine goblet in the correct way.
9) Irene gulps down the wine.
10) Katherine blurts out that she doesn't really like the food, which makes Rita embarrassed.
11) Irene wants to leave before the luncheon comes to an end.

2. Read the poem *Invitation to Wine* (Li Bai, translated by Xu Yuanchong), and then discuss the following questions with your group members.

Key for reference:

1) "劝酒" (Invite or urge sb. to drink) is very important in Chinese wine culture, and it is almost a kind of etiquette. Wine is indispensable at a Chinese meal, no matter whether it is formal or informal, a banquet or a family reunion dinner. The host, hostess and guests usually toast or invite others to drink which shows they respect or value each other.

2) Students can answer this question in Chinese and especially give the examples of poems 《送元二使安西》,《水调歌头·明月几时有》,《短歌行》,《月下独酌》, etc. Since ancient times in China, poetry and wine have been combined together. Whether it is a celebration or a banquet, it is necessary to offer wine and recite poems. Over time, it gradually formed a special cultural custom: poetry and wine often combine together. With wine, poetry becomes more wonderful: with poetry, wine becomes more mellow. Therefore, Chinese literati like drinking and for some of them, drinking can inspire them and wine can help them to express their feelings.

Module Four

Chapter One Etiquette in Job Interview

Warm-up:

Who do you think will receive the offer of employment at last?

Key for reference:

MIRANDA is the most likely to get the offer.

As newbies, the three college graduates don't have much work experience, and what they are applying for is a common administrative position.

Hanna's question is critical, concerning a lot about the countermeasures of the top management to cope with the risks, which is considered an arrogation to the high power.

Raising no question doesn't mean that Jaden knows everything well. Actually, it is not wise to hold back all the questions in this last session of the interview. One or two questions are a best choice.

Miranda's question focuses on the criteria of a qualified staff of the company. It shows that she cares much about how to do well in her duties and hopes to get further development in this job.

Exercise

2. Case study

Case 1: According to the case, do you think Zhang Lili will pass the interview? If not, what are the possible causes?

Key for reference:

Zhang Lili's chances of passing the interview will be greatly reduced or even lost because of her hesitation. Employees who do not have an opinion are generally not welcome. Over-dependence on parents is a common problem for some college students. Remember, after going into society one has to learn to be independent. Relying on parents for everything is difficult to gain the trust of employers.

Case 2: Please analyze the reasons for the failure of Xiao Qiang's interview.

Key for reference:

The reason why Xiaoqiang failed the interview was that the company felt he lacked teamwork spirit. Colleagues must do a good job of communication, and close cooperation can make the company's business run efficiently. Self-confidence and pride are sometimes in the line between, and pride is annoying. People without team spirit or unable to fit in with groups are difficult to be favored by employers. After all, modern enterprises will not like a lone range.

Chapter Two Business Conference Etiquette

Exercise

2. Case study

Case 1

Issues to discuss: 1) What are the complaints? How to deal with them?

2) If you are the liaison man, what will you do? What is your reception plan?

Key for reference:

1) Students can answer questions according to their own analysis of the case.

2) If you encounter similar problems in the reception of foreign guests, the first principle is to find a solution as soon as possible and send the guests to the designated place. Suggestions for the follow-up treatment are as follows. First, sincerely apologize for the mistakes in vehicle arrangement again, and make a reasonable explanation for such problems. Be neither humble nor pushy, but dignified and gracious. And don't try to cover up the problems. Second, discuss your advice with all the guests present, and arrange some passengers to take the originally arranged vehicles. Third, you can immediately call the online taxi-hailing service to arrange for the rest of the guests to leave. Fourth, please ask the organizing committee to arrange cars to transport luggage.

Case 2

Read the news report on the PR crisis that BMW Mini faced because of their staff's misbehavior in their booth at auto show and discuss:

1) What were the problems with the booth staff in BMW mini booth?

Key for reference:

a. Its employees' dereliction of duty. Their behavior involved suspected discrimination against Chinese visitors at the Shanghai auto show, which could not be tolerated. Staff in the booth should be friendly to every visitor and treat every visitor equally.

b. Food and drinks were provided to the booth staff in the trade fair. According to the apology issued by the company after this PR crisis, the ice cream was provided not only to the visitors, but also to the staff (referring to the foreign visitors who got the ice cream). However, one of the most common trade show booth etiquette violations occurs when food and drink are kept in the booth for the staff's personal consumption. Snacks and drinks should not be consumed in the booth or left visible to trade show attendees.

2) Some observers believed that rather than discrimination against Chinese people, the incident demonstrated the xenophilia that still exists in Chinese society. To what extent do you agree with the statement?

Key for reference:

The mood of the nation is an important element of a country's comprehensive strength and a motivation to the development of a country. As China is approaching to the center of the world and making greater contributions to human being, promoting the well-rounded development of all our people and building the mood of the nation that matches China's comprehensive strength are crucial. It is necessary to nurture rational patriots who have a broad global vision, a mind of great power and are able to express love for the country rationally and legally, so that Chinese people are well-prepared to oppose to xenophilia and self-humiliation, as well as xenophobia and overassertion.

Chapter Three Etiquette in a Business Ceremony

I. Signing Ceremony

Warm-up:

Scan the QR code to watch the following video and try to find out the mistakes in the signing ceremony.

Key for reference:

Mistake 1: The host has the wrong seating arrangement. The Thai guest should be seated on the right side of the host.

Mistake 2: Stanley, the Thai representative, dresses himself too casually.

Mistake 3: Amber, the Chinese representative, passes the contract with her left hand.

Mistake 4: The Chinese company sends a gift without package to the Thai guests.

II. Ribbon-cutting Ceremony

Warm-up:

Key for reference:

The following ones are proper: 2, 6, 8.

Reference 参考文献

1. Jacqueline Whitmore. *Business Class Etiquette Essentials for Success at Work*［M］. 姜岩，译. 北京：中央编译出版社，2010.
2. 崔海潮. 商务礼仪（第 2 版）［M］. 北京：北京师范大学出版社，2018.
3. 韩振华. 商务礼仪［M］. 杭州：浙江大学出版社，2022.
4. 胡小伟. 中国酒文化［M］. 北京：中国国际广播出版社，2020.
5. 金正昆. 礼仪金说［M］. 西安：陕西师范大学出版社，2006.
6. 金正昆. 商务礼仪教程（第四版）［M］. 北京：中国人民大学出版社，2013.
7. 金正昆，孙燕. 公务礼仪［M］. 北京：华文出版社，2013.
8. 李爽，李阳. 商务礼仪实务［M］. 北京：清华大学出版社，2017.
9. 李永生，杜琳. 涉外交际礼仪［M］. 北京：外语教学与研究出版社，2016.
10. 舒静庐. 礼仪天下：会议礼仪［M］. 上海：上海三联书店，2014.
11. 万里红. 最实战商务礼仪［M］. 北京：机械工业出版社，2012.
12. 万文斌，郝素玲，陈明华. 商务礼仪［M］. 北京：航空工业出版社，2012.
13. 王琳. 唐装的穿着搭配［J］. 现代国际，2003（1）：65.
14. 魏凯林. 实用商务礼仪［M］. 北京：清华大学出版社，2017.
15. 吴晓路. 国际商务礼仪［M］. 北京：中国纺织出版社，2018.
16. 杨茳. 礼仪师培训教程［M］. 北京：人民交通出版社，2007.
17. 于丽萍. 中国传统礼仪文化的当代价值及其实现机制研究［D］. 山东大学，2016.4.
18. 于立新. 国际商务礼仪实训（第三版）［M］. 北京：对外经济贸易大学出版社，2018.
19. 张宇，艾天姿. 国际商务礼仪英文教程［M］. 北京：北京大学出版社，2012.
20. 周国宝. 现代国际礼仪（英文版）［M］. 北京：北京师范大学出版社，2014.
21. 邹亮，王颖. 实用商务礼仪［M］. 北京：北京理工大学出版社，2017.
22. 茱莉亚. 有礼行天下：茱莉亚的职场礼仪精华课［M］. 北京：中国青年出版社，2015.
23. 朱亚楠，周洪梅. 浅析中山装的形制及文化理念［J］. 山东纺织经济，2019（5）：18.